THEORIES OF ECONOMIC GROWTH AND DEVELOPMENT

IRMA ADELMAN

THEORIES OF ECONOMIC GROWTH AND DEVELOPMENT

STANFORD UNIVERSITY PRESS
STANFORD, CALIFORNIA
LONDON: OXFORD UNIVERSITY PRESS 1962

Stanford University Press
Stanford, California
London: Oxford University Press

Printed in the United States of America

To the memory of my father

PREFACE

IN THE HALF-CENTURY prior to World War II, the major concern of economists was with static, short-run, equilibrium analysis. The theories of consumer demand, of equilibrium of the firm, of income distribution, and of resource allocation were refined with the aid of these concepts. Even trade-cycle analysis and the theory of employment evolved within a largely short-run equilibrium framework.

Since then, the problems of economic growth and development have been thrust upon the current generation of economists by a world intent on economic progress. In the last two decades, nations have become increasingly development-oriented. Economic development is now a major issue in international politics. As a result, just as in the nineteenth century, long-run economic dynamics has once more become a primary concern of the profession.

Perhaps the major function of this study is to examine, in the context of modern economic theory and with the aid of modern economic tools, the evolution of economic thought in the field of growth and development. The second chapter presents a rather general mathematical schema, which forms the basis of the remainder of the book. In the succeeding four chapters the general framework is used to clarify the basic assumptions and conclusions inherent in the theories of economic growth of Smith, Ricardo, Marx, and Schumpeter. Finally, a modern model of economic development is presented, and some conclusions are drawn concerning the nature of economic development policies in a modern underdeveloped society.

The present work is an outgrowth of my collaboration with Adamantios Pepelasis and Leon Mears on an undergraduate textbook in economic development. I am very grateful to both of them for their help and encouragement in the early stages of this book.

My greatest personal debt is to Frank L. Adelman, my severest and most exacting critic, whose dual role as patient husband and less patient inculcator of precision and logic has contributed significantly to both the quality and preparation time of this book. I must also express my deep appreciation to Robert Dorfman, whose insistence on the scientific method and whose qualities as teacher and economist have exerted a strong and continuing influence upon my professional development.

The stimulation offered by Nicholas Kaldor, F. H. Hahn, H. B. Chenery, and the members of Professor Kaldor's seminar at Berkeley during the period in which the major portion of this book was written cannot be overestimated. Further improvements in the manuscript are due directly to the many helpful comments offered by Moses Abramovitz, K. J. Arrow, P. A. Baran, B. F. Haley, John Green, H. P. Minsky, Gustav Ranis, Henry Rosovsky, Aubrey Silberston, Stephen Sosnick, Donald Winch, Hirofumi Uzawa, and the Stanford University Press referee. In addition, the framework of Chapter Two was strongly influenced by T. Haavelmo, *A Study in the Theory of Economic Evolution.* Finally, I am very grateful to Dr. E. K. Bauer and the editorial staff of Stanford University Press for their excellent editorial assistance. Part of the preparation cost of the manuscript was borne by the Stanford Project for Quantitative Research in Economic Development, which is financed by the Ford Foundation.

I wish also to thank Harper & Brothers for their permission to quote from Schumpeter, *Capitalism, Socialism and Democracy* (New York, 1950); Harvard University Press for their permission to reprint excerpts from Joseph A. Schumpeter, *The Theory of Economic Development* (Cambridge, Mass.: Harvard University Press), Copyright 1934 by the President and Fellows of Harvard College; and McGraw-Hill for their permission to quote from Schumpeter, *Business Cycles* (New York, 1939).

I. A.

Stanford, California
September 1961

CONTENTS

ONE

INTRODUCTION

AN ADEQUATE DEFINITION of economic development is not easy to construct. The vast disparities in natural endowments, economic structure, cultural heritage, and social and political institutions that exist between different regions of the world today are likely to invalidate any attempt to devise a single criterion for distinguishing "developed" from "underdeveloped" countries. Even definitional approaches that combine a number of indicators of economic underdevelopment have so far proved intellectually unsatisfactory because they include so many variables that they become descriptive rather than analytical in character.[1] As a result, a division of the world into "developed" and "underdeveloped" segments is more or less arbitrary and can be achieved only at the cost of great complexity or gross oversimplification.

Nevertheless, definitions are necessary to establish ground rules for discussion. In this book we shall define economic development as the process by which an economy is transformed from one whose rate of growth of per capita income is small or negative to one in which a significant self-sustained rate of increase of per capita income is a permanent long-run feature. A society will be called underdeveloped if economic development is possible but incomplete.

This definition of economic development appears to be a reasonable one. It does not describe an empty set, since in the Western capitalist economies (since the Industrial Revolution) a persistent, endogenously generated rise in the rate of growth of per capita output has taken place, and this growth rate has remained significantly positive for an extended period of time. On the other hand, our definition serves to distinguish economic development from such processes as sporadic growth and growth sustained primarily by exogenous forces.

With regard to our definition of an underdeveloped economy, it should be pointed out that it is in no sense a "single criterion" definition.

On the contrary, our assignment of an economy to the category of "underdeveloped" must be predicated upon a rather complete examination of its economic and socio-cultural behavioral relationships. Only on this broad basis can we determine whether economic development is (1) possible, (2) in progress, or (3) essentially complete.

Before we begin our study of the interactions governing long-run economic behavior, it may prove useful to point out some of the features of the current economic scene that lend a sense of urgency to the problem of development. Foremost among these is the tremendous difference in per capita real national income that exists between rich countries and poor. This disparity is quite evident from the Table (pp. 4 and 5). Column (1) gives the average per capita income in 52 countries for the period from 1952 to 1954, converted into 1953 U.S. dollars with the aid of exchange rates adjusted for local differences in purchasing power. The low levels of per capita income in much of the world indicate the magnitude of the economic problem ahead. Indeed, it would appear that two-thirds of the world's population lives at a bare subsistence level.[2]

Admittedly, intercountry comparisons of per capita incomes are, at best, only rough indicators of relative levels of community welfare.[3] First of all, national income statistics do not include all of the flows of goods and services in a community. They exclude barter transactions and much of the economic activity represented by home-produced, home-consumed output, and they do not take into account the domestic services of housewives, the services of consumer durables, or the services of social overhead capital. In addition, national income comparisons of this nature cannot reflect adequately any of the non-material contributions of the society to the welfare of its people.

Next, the internal inconsistency of national income estimates[4] and the distortions created by the use of exchange rates[5] (adjusted, in some sense or other, for differences in the relative costs of living) introduce a fair degree of arbitrariness into the results. And, finally, the use of per capita income figures (which constitute averages over the community) tends to conceal the large difference in the composition of output and in the distribution of income among the various members of the society.*

---

* This last defect will also be present in the later chapters of this book.

In spite of these deficiencies of national income comparisons, however, the differences between nations are so big that even indicators of national welfare as crude as those derived from the currently available data on per capita incomes can serve as useful guides to the size of the required gains and as qualitative measures of economic progress.

Large as the existing national income disparities are, one can expect the development of further inequities for some years to come. Columns (2) and (3) of the Table give relevant information on estimated short-run and long-run rates of growth of per capita income. From the short-run figures it is evident that many of the poorer countries are essentially stagnant and cannot even begin to narrow the income gap without significant changes in their way of economic life.

Of course, the long-run rate of growth is the most important for our discussion, since our definitions of economic development and underdevelopment hinge upon the behavior of this quantity. Unfortunately, relatively few data exist on long-run rates of growth, but what evidence we have suggests that the more opulent societies are the ones which are growing more rapidly.

A number of other quantities often used as indicators of economic development are presented in the Table. These include such economic variables as the proportion of the labor force engaged in primary activities (column 6) and the ratio of foreign trade to the gross domestic product (column 9), both of which are negatively correlated with per capita income, and economic characteristics like the share of value added in manufacturing (column 5), the capital–labor ratio in manufacturing (column 7), and the percentage of investment (column 4), all of which are positively correlated with per capita income. In addition, several important demographic and socio-cultural features are tabulated for most of the countries listed. In the socio-cultural sphere, it is apparent that both literacy (column 10) and urbanization (column 11) increase as per capita income goes up; with regard to the demographic features, lower incomes are generally associated with higher crude birth and death rates (columns 12 and 13), larger infant mortality (column 14), and reduced life expectancy (columns 15 and 16).

Naturally, the relationships noted above are not perfect. In Chile, Venezuela, and Bolivia, for example, a high per capita income (relative to the degree of industrialization) has been reached by reliance on extractive industry, whereas New Zealand, Argentina, and Puerto Rico

PER CAPITA INCOME AND OTHER ECONOMIC

(Date is 1953 except

Countries	(1) Per cap. income 1953 U.S. $	(2) Short-run % rate of growth per cap. income	(3) Long-run % rate of growth per cap. income	(4) Invest-ment as a % of nat'l income	(5) Value added by mfg. as % total val. add.	(6) Agr'l labor as % of total labor force	(7) Capacity installed per person engaged (horse-power)
United States	1855.5	1.8	16.4	18.9	32.3	12.2[c]	7.53
New Zealand	1322.0	—0.9	11.8	20.4	21.4	18.4[c]	5.49
Canada	1299.2	1.4	17.0	28.4	29.1	19.1[c]	7.84
United Kingdom	1121.5	2.1	11.0	16.4	34.6	5.2[c]	4.76
Australia	1071.7	—2.8	9.5	29.3	31.0	15.6[b]	3.87
Sweden	1045.8	2.5	29.2	20.9	19.0	20.4[c]	6.95
Switzerland	1022.3	3.5	15.3	22.3	40.1	16.5[c]	4.21
Luxemburg	895.7	0.8	....	27.6	35.8	....	4.38
Denmark	795.2	1.7	16.7	22.2	27.7	25.1[c]	3.46
Belgium	734.8	2.9	....	16.6	32.1	12.5[b]	3.15
Norway	715.1	2.3	23.4	32.0	27.5	25.9[c]	6.33
France	685.6	4.0	10.4	19.6	32.2	36.5[b]	2.72
Germany, Fed. Rep.	603.2	7.1	8.3	25.2	37.6	23.2[c]	3.43
Venezuela	530.5	8.0	....	20.9	10.0	41.3[c]	3.84
Finland	490.2	3.3	....	28.1	31.9	46.0[c]	5.99
Netherlands	488.9	3.8	9.0	22.9	30.2	19.7[b]	2.94
Argentina	460.0	—0.4	....	17.0	19.7	25.2[b]	2.10
Union of S. Africa	456.4	0.6	23.8	26.1	29.0	48.3[b]	2.82
Austria	444.0	6.2	....	19.0	43.2	32.1[c]	2.82
Puerto Rico	411.9	3.6	....	20.1	19.3	37.1[c]	3.14
Ireland	403.3	1.5	16.3	18.3	27.6	39.6[c]	3.25
Chile	359.1	—0.3	....	13.3	12.8	30.1[c]	2.06
Spain	335.6	5.2	5.6	19.5	22.3	48.8[c]	....
Italy	309.8	5.2	14.2	22.1	31.9	41.2[c]	2.89
Costa Rica	268.1	2.7	....	23.5	11.2	55.0[c]	2.14
Mexico	230.1	2.8	....	13.0	24.1	58.3[c]	2.46
Brazil	230.0	2.5	....	15.7	24.5	60.6[c]	2.01
Turkey	208.6	3.6	....	13.7	10.9	85.7[c]	2.54
Fed. Rhod. & Nyas'l'd	200.2	2.7	....	32.5	18.4	....	....
Yugoslavia	196.0	8.8	....	32.0	42.4	66.8	2.60
Colombia	187.4	2.8	....	14.1	15.7	72.7[a]	2.00
Dominican Republic	186.4	3.9	....	15.5	17.1	....	2.10
Japan	181.0	6.7	21.7	31.1	31.9	48.4[c]	2.75
Portugal	172.3	3.4	....	17.9	34.7	48.4[c]	1.67
Greece	170.6	6.8	....	17.3	18.9	....	1.03
Honduras	153.0	2.2	....	17.5	8.8	83.2[c]	0.48
Peru	145.0	0.0	....	26.3	14.4	62.5[b]	2.44
Guatemala	143.6	1.2	....	9.6	15.1	....	1.58
Paraguay	140.0	1.4	....	....	19.4	55.4[c]	1.28
Ecuador	129.2	2.0	....	15.0	17.9	49.4[c]	2.38
Egypt	118.1	0.6	....	12.2	11.3	59.7[b]	1.84
Ceylon	112.1	0.4	....	11.2	5.3	52.9[b]	1.75
South Korea	104.5	4.1	....	11.5	7.2	....	1.84
Thailand	82.0	2.3	....	....	12.3	84.8[b]	1.56
Philippines	74.5	4.2	....	8.7	11.7	71.3[b]	1.84
Bolivia	68.5	—40.5	....	10.5	3.7	72.1[c]	....
Belgian Congo	62.1	3.4	....	32.0	14.2	84.9[c]	....
China-Taiwan	57.2	4.7	....	20.4	24.7	....	1.38
India	57.1	1.6	....	....	17.0	70.6[c]	1.67
Pakistan	51.4	0.3	....	....	8.8	76.5[c]	1.64
Indonesia	50.7	5.0	....	....	6.7	....	1.52
Burma	48.5	5.6	....	20.4	9.5	....	1.74

(*a*) Year or years during period 1930–39; (*b*) Year or years during period 1940–49; (*c*) Year or years during period 1950–59.

(1) Per capita income, 1953, U.S. dollars from *Yearbook of National Accounts Statistics,* 1958, U.N. exchange rates from "Patterns of Industrial Growth," U.N., 1960. (2) Short-run rate of growth per capita income derived from (1). (3) Long-run rate of growth per capita income from Kuznets, S., "Percent Change per Decade National Product per Capita, Constant Prices, First Half of Twentieth Century," in *Economic Development and Cultural Change,* Oct. 1956. (4) Investment as per cent of national income, from *Yearbook of National Accounts Statistics, op. cit.* (5) Value added by manufacturing as per cent total value added from *Yearbook of National Accounts Statistics, op. cit.,* and "Gross Domestic Product by Sectors of Origin, 1953," U.N., dittoed. (6) Agricultural labor as per cent of total labor force from Kuznets, S., *Econ.*

CHARACTERISTICS OF FIFTY-TWO NATIONS

where otherwise noted)

(8)	(9)	(10)	(11)	(12)	(13)	(14)	(15)	(15)
Relative productivity of agriculture	Exports + imports as % of nat'l income	Literacy index	Urbanization index	Crude birth rate	Crude death rate	Infant mortality rates	Life expectancy at birth	
							Male	Fem.
0.59[c]	9.4	....	35.3[c]	24.6	9.6	27.8	68.6	
1.56[c]	63.2	....	41.6[c]	25.4	9.0	25.7	68.3[c]	72.4[c]
0.68[c]	47.6	....	27.5[c]	28.2	8.6	35.4	66.3[c]	70.8[c]
1.08[c]	46.4	....	59.5[c]	15.9	11.4	27.6	67.3	72.4
0.82[a]	42.4	....	48.4[a]	22.9	9.1	23.3	66.1[b]	70.6[b]
0.63[c]	55.7	....	25.4[c]	15.4	9.7	18.7	69.0[b]	71.6[b]
....	59.0	....	24.8[c]	17.0	10.2	29.8	62.7[b]	67.0[b]
....	159.4	....	21.3[b]	16.0	12.5	41.7	61.7[b]	65.8[b]
0.82[c]	66.5	....	36.7[c]	17.9	9.0	27.2	67.8[b]	70.1[b]
0.66[b]	63.0	96.9[b]	17.9[b]	16.6	12.1	41.9	62.0[b]	67.3[b]
0.58[c]	89.2	....	26.0[c]	18.7	8.5	22.0	69.3[b]	72.7[b]
0.47[b]	31.9	92.7[b]	23.1[c]	18.9	13.1	41.9	63.6[c]	69.3[c]
0.50[c]	37.9	....	32.7[c]	15.5	11.0	46.2	64.6[c]	68.5[c]
....	60.6	48.9[c]	21.8[c]	....	....	....	....	....
0.57[c]	45.8	....	14.2[c]	21.9	9.6	34.2	62.9[c]	69.1[c]
0.66[b]	104.3	....	41.3[b]	21.8	7.7	22.1	70.6[c]	72.9[c]
0.72[b]	12.2	86.7[b]	42.1[b]	24.7	8.7	....	56.9[b]	61.4[b]
0.32[b]	43.0	27.0[b]	28.2[c]	25.7	8.9	34.1	63.8[b]	68.3[b]
0.49[c]	44.3	....	35.2[c]	14.8	12.0	49.9	61.9[c]	67.0[c]
0.53[c]	129.3	74.4[c]	23.3[c]	35.1	....	....	....	....
0.82[c]	80.7	....	23.7[c]	21.2	11.7	39.4	60.5[b]	62.4[b]
0.55[c]	18.2	....	27.3[b]	34.6	12.4	112.4	49.8[c]	53.9[c]
....	13.1	....	28.3[c]	20.6	9.7	58.9	47.1[b]	53.2[b]
0.64[c]	28.5	....	28.0[c]	17.7	10.1	58.4	57.5[a]	....
....	64.1	78.8[c]	17.5[c]	....	....	....	55.7[c]	
0.32[c]	31.1	....	13.6[b]	45.0	15.9	95.2	37.9[b]	39.8[b]
0.56[c]	16.2	48.4[c]	16.3[c]	....	....	....	49.8[c]	56.0[c]
0.57[c]	17.0	34.3[c]	10.1[c]	....	....	....	....	....
....	109.6	....	0[c]	27.6	6.2	25.2	....	....
0.43[c]	15.4	74.6[b]	8.1[b]	28.4	12.4	116.3	....	....
....	33.8	....	....	....	....	....	....	....
....	44.1	43.2[c]	11.1[c]	....	....	....	....	....
0.50[c]	27.8	....	33.3[c]	21.5	8.9	48.9	61.9	65.7
0.60[c]	38.9	58.2[c]	12.7[c]	23.4	11.3	95.5	55.5[c]	60.5[c]
....	29.0	76.1[c]	16.2[c]	....	....	....	....	....
0.67[c]	50.5	33.7[b]	5.3[c]	....	11.0	87.4	....	....
0.57[b]	48.5	....	....	....	....	....	....	....
....	47.0	29.7[c]	10.2[c]	51.1	23.2	103.0	36.0[b]	37.1[b]
0.86[c]	....	68.2[c]	15.2[c]	....	....	....	....	....
0.81[c]	38.6	56.3[c]	14.6[c]	....	....	....	....	....
0.58[b]	40.4	22.1[b]	22.7[b]	....	....	....	35.7[a]	41.5[a]
1.03[b]	80.3	63.8[b]	8.8[b]	39.4	10.9	71.2	57.6[c]	55.5[c]
....	16.7	....	....	....	....	....	....	....
0.64[b]	....	53.7[b]	57.4[b]	....	....	....	48.7[b]	51.9[b]
0.57[b]	30.2	59.8[b]	17.6[b]	....	....	....	....	....
0.77[c]	72.9	31.1[c]	....	....	....	....	....	....
0.39[c]	85.7	....	....	....	....	....	37.6[c]	40.0[c]
....	28.8	....	....	45.3	9.5	33.7	41.1[a]	45.7[a]
0.71[c]	....	19.9[c]	8.7[c]	....	....	....	32.5[b]	31.7[b]
0.79[c]	....	....	....	....	....	....	....	....
....	....	....	....	....	....	....	....	....
....	56.1	....	....	....	....	....	....	....

Development and Cultural Change, July 1957. (7) Capacity installed per person engaged, *Patterns of Industrial Growth, op. cit.* (8) Product per worker including family labor in current prices, Kuznets, S., July 1957, *op. cit.* (9) Foreign trade as per cent of national income from *Yearbook of National Accounts Statistics, op. cit.* (10) Literacy index from *Demographic Yearbook, 1955,* U.N., per cent population 10 years and over with ability to read and to write. (11) Urbanization index, *ibid.,* except Australia, Chile, Mexico from *World Population and Production,* Woytinsky, W. S., and E. S., Twentieth Century Fund, 1953, per cent population in places with population greater than 50,000. (12) Crude birth rates from *Statistical Yearbook, 1956,* U.N., number of live births per 1000 population. (13) Crude death rates, *ibid.,* number of deaths per 1000 population. (14) Infant mortality rates, *ibid.,* number of deaths of infants under one year age per 1000 live births. (15) Life expectancy at birth, male, *ibid.* (16) Life expectancy at birth, female, *ibid.*

have achieved a similar result with the aid of extensive commercial agriculture as a substitute for manufacturing activity. On the other hand, because of rather meager resource endowments, per capita incomes in Switzerland and Japan are lower than would be warranted by their degree of industrialization. And in Yugoslavia and Nationalist China, the full impact of the post–World War II industrialization efforts upon per capita standards of living had certainly not made itself felt by 1953.

There are a number of other exceptions to the general relationships that can be derived from the Table. Some, of course, can be explained quite easily in terms of abnormal features of the society in question. Others may require more subtle analysis to determine the reasons for departure from the general patterns. In any case, the existence of such anomalies suggests that in the absence of a sound theoretical foundation the analysis of empirical data cannot be relied upon to lead to universal conclusions about the causes and paths of economic growth. Specifically, multiple correlation studies, one of the mainstays of the empirical approach, indicate mutual association at most, and offer no intimation of cause or effect. Indeed, they occasionally lead even a sophisticated economist to spurious relationships. Observational evidence and empirical analysis, of course, often provide invaluable direction to theory, but the very abundance of variables that can affect economic development makes it difficult to determine just which of the parameters of a developing society are the significant ones. It follows, therefore, that strong theoretical guidance is a necessary prerequisite to describe sensibly the phenomena of economic development. In addition, a good theoretical model would permit valid generalizations from one specific economic situation to another, and would greatly assist in the formulation of sound economic policy.

In the next chapter we shall present a rather general theoretical framework from which we shall later attempt to adduce a common explanation for the growth patterns of various economic systems. Our task will be to present a dynamic analysis of economic development that is sufficiently broad to permit us to encompass both the phenomenon of self-sustained progress and that of economic stagnation. In short, we shall again address ourselves to the classical economic problem that is so neatly summarized in the full title of Adam Smith's treatise—*An*

Inquiry into the Nature and Causes of the Wealth of Nations. The framework of Chapter Two is intended to be a systemization of past and current economic thought about the evolution of an economy, and each economist will recognize therein many elements of his own point of view. Of necessity, we shall not be specific in this chapter; that is, we shall present neither a *theory* of growth nor a *model* of a growing economy. Rather, to analyze economic development we shall formulate a structure[6] that will be sufficiently general to permit us to treat the theories of a number of economists as particular special cases. Although this structure will not in itself permit us to draw immediate conclusions concerning the nature of the growth-promoting and growth-inhibiting forces in an economy, it will serve to channel our thinking along specific lines of inquiry into this question.

In the subsequent chapters we shall analyze in detail with the aid of the framework of Chapter Two the long-run dynamic behavior of economic systems as seen by Smith, Ricardo, Marx, Schumpeter, and the Neo-Keynesians. Then we shall see, in Chapter Eight, what common conclusions and recommendations can be derived from a reasonable synthesis of the doctrines of the authors we have discussed. Our major objectives are first to see to what extent a clearer picture of economic development can be derived, and second to suggest, if possible, reasonable policies whose implementation may speed development.

TWO

A GENERAL FRAMEWORK FOR ANALYSIS

THE ANALYSIS PRESENTED in this chapter will use, as the fundamental criterion of economic development, the total output of the economy. This implies that, for our present purposes, we are willing to accept both (1) the deficiencies associated with the use of flows of market-oriented products as indicators of comparative development, and (2) the complexities of the several welfare and index-number problems associated with the use of this concept. If some other yardsticks, such as the per capita output or the rate of growth of either per capita or total output,[1] should seem more appropriate to the reader, he may still use our analysis without modification; he need merely apply his own set of criteria at the end to draw his conclusions.

Using the economy's output level as an index of the stage of economic development suggests that the production function is the keystone of our structure. This function relates the economy's output rate at time t (Y_t)* to the quantities of various inputs actually used in production and to the major forces conditioning the productivity of production factors.† Given the state of technology and the institutional

---

* The subscript "t" is used to denote the value of the variable at time t.

† This definition of the production function differs from the usual one. The conventional production function is a relationship between inputs and output only. The influence of the factors that condition the productivity of the physical inputs (e.g., technology and the socio-economic environment) is usually subsumed in the shape of the production function. Hence, in the usual treatment exogenous changes in the shape of the production function are used to portray the effects of technological and environmental forces. For greater generality, we prefer to keep the shape of the production function independent of time and to provide the possibility for an endogenous treatment of technological and social factors. Note, however, that the conventional approach is merely a special case of our structure.

and socio-cultural environment of the community, the production function represents the maximum amount of output obtainable with each combination of the physical inputs. Since we assume implicitly that the institutional and economic environments determine uniquely the allocation of resources among the various firms, the usual hypothesis that each firm will operate to produce the maximum possible output with the available inputs results in our specifying, in effect, that the economy itself, at each point of the production function, is manufacturing the largest amount of goods it can produce with the given amounts and allocation of factors and the level of technology of the society.

We shall therefore take our production function to be

$$Y_t = f(K_t, N_t, L_t, S_t, U_t)\,, \tag{2.1}$$

where K_t denotes the amount of the services of the economy's capital stock employed at time t, N_t stands for the rate of use of natural resources, and L_t represents the employment of the labor force. In order to deal more easily with factor productivity variations stemming from technological innovations and from changes in the skills of the labor force, we have introduced into our production function the symbol S_t, which represents the society's fund of applied knowledge.[2] The same thing could have been accomplished, of course, by making the shape of the production function itself time-dependent. From a mathematical point of view, however, it is simpler to define the shape of the production function f to be independent of time, as in (2.1). Similarly, in order to treat (at least in principle) the impact of social, cultural, and institutional changes upon the productivity of the economy, we also include in our production function a symbol U_t, which represents the socio-cultural milieu within which the economy operates.* Thus, we recognize explicitly that the output rate of an economy is not a purely economic phenomenon.[3]

Let us consider briefly each of the economic inputs in turn. The evaluation of the stock of capital (K_t) raises very difficult problems both in principle and in practice.[4] These problems stem primarily from the incommensurability of different types of physical products. Quan-

* Production function (2.1) does not imply that the variables K_t, N_t, L_t, S_t, and U_t are independent of each other. Indeed, in equations (2.3)–(2.7) the rates of change of each of these variables are related to all other variables in the system.

tification of capital wealth is generally achieved, therefore, by using the money values of real assets. These are derived on the basis of either the (adjusted) historical cost of the capital equipment, the (modified) replacement cost, or the (estimated) capitalized earning power of the physical assets. In an economy in which the techniques of production, the composition of output, and the characteristics of the labor force all change through time, however, estimates of the capital stock of the economy on any of these bases can be no more than a rough but educated guess. For there exists an interdependence between the evaluation of the capital stock at any point of time and the specific future time path assumed for the other economic variables of the system. In particular, the measurement of the economy's capital depends upon the nature of our postulates concerning the type and rate of technological progress.[5] (With no innovations, for example, there is no obsolescence of capital equipment, and hence the adjustment of historical costs need take account only of physical wear and tear of assets and of changes in price level.) Regardless of these difficulties of measurement, however, all economic theories of growth to date have used either the capital stock of the economy or the rate of investment as one of the crucial variables in the system.

While capital is thus often regarded as a basic determinant of economic growth, natural resources (N_t) are seldom considered to be as important.* Since, by definition, natural resources consist of non-reproducible assets, many economists consider the natural wealth of an economy to be constant through time. Others combine both the reproducible and non-reproducible forms of material wealth into a single portmanteau variable—capital.[6] In any case, the evaluation of N_t is fully as complex as that of K_t, since all the quantification difficulties mentioned in our discussion of the capital stock carry over also into the measurement of N_t, and, in addition, adequate resource surveys exist for only a very few of the more developed nations.

The labor component (L_t) of our central relationship (2.1) would appear, at first glance, to be homogeneous.[7] However, a little reflection will reveal that it too is a conglomerate of incommensurate entities. Dissimilarities in skills among the several grades of labor and varia-

* The Physiocrats are, of course, notable exceptions to this statement.

tions (both in time and in location) in the efficiency of the same grade of labor make a meaningful evaluation of the size of the work force an undertaking much more complex than a mere nose-count. Furthermore, both the quality and the composition of the labor force vary through time and are not independent of the rates of change of the other variables in the system. Specifically, changes in the skills and health of the labor force are directly dependent upon changes in the society's applied fund of technical knowledge (S_t). And, by the same token, cultural and institutional variations in the labor force cannot be divorced from differences in the socio-cultural environment (U_t).

The conceptual problems which arise from the heterogeneity and incommensurability of the production factors may be reduced somewhat if we think of each input as a multicomponent vector rather than as a single number. Therefore, we define the economy's capital stock as

$$K_t = (K_{1t}, K_{2t}, \ldots, K_{jt}, \ldots, K_{pt}),$$

where K_{jt} is the amount of the jth type of capital equipment in use at time t. Similarly, we write

$$N_t = (N_{1t}, N_{2t}, \ldots, N_{jt}, \ldots, N_{qt}),$$

and

$$L_t = (L_{1t}, L_{2t}, \ldots, L_{jt}, \ldots, L_{rt}).$$

In the above expressions N_{jt} and L_{jt} are the quantity of the jth kind of natural resource and the amount of the jth grade of labor employed at time t, respectively. This procedure permits us to disaggregate each input any time we feel it is desirable and practicable to do so. Of course, unless K_t, N_t, and L_t are to be minutely detailed inventory lists, the index-number problems inherent in the quantification of these concepts are merely pushed back one step further; they are not entirely eliminated.

Even more difficult than the measurement problems raised by the three production factors are those posed by an attempt to quantify our last two variables. S_t and U_t represent heuristic devices, introduced primarily for conceptual purposes. They symbolize forces whose role in development is undoubtedly vital, but whose quantification is possible, at best, only in an ordinal sense. (For our purposes this is all that is required, however.) Therefore, even in principle, these last two variables cannot, at present, be placed on a footing equivalent to that of the physical inputs. At some time in the future a method may be devised for the ordinal evaluation of S_t and U_t, but such a method does not now exist, and accordingly neither variable can be used as an analytic tool. Consequently, the symbols S_t and U_t are to be viewed merely as shorthand expressions for two very complex sets of factors and phenomena that condition economic progress. One may hope, however, that, as social scientists gain a better insight into the relevant dimensions of these two classes of forces, a judicious choice of indicators may permit a rough ordinal evaluation of S_t and U_t. Our framework suggests how one could then use these concepts in economic analysis.

The variable S_t is a Schumpeterian type of quantity representing the society's fund of applied scientific, technical, and organizational knowledge.[8] Like the physical inputs, S_t is a multidimensional vector, each of whose v components is an index of the level of a particular kind of technical, organizational, or scientific skill in use at time t.* The explicit introduction of S_t into the production function permits us to analyze changes in the productivity of land, labor, and capital which are not due to quantitative variations in their rate of use. For, with the aid of this variable, we can take into account the effect upon the economy of such factors as changes in technology and improvements in the skills and health of the labor force. It is true that the impact of changes in S_t upon output can be felt only through the influence of technological forces upon the productivity of the physical inputs. One immediate effect of such changes in productivity will be to vary the total amounts

---

* Conceptually, to specify the vector S_t, we must draw up for any given line of production a list of techniques in use. For every amount of a specified output, each technique provides us with a detailed blueprint of a productive process and specifies the required amounts of the particular types of capital equipment, raw material, semi-finished products, and grades of labor. Of course, given relative factor prices, there is at each point of time a minimum production cost technique for each amount of a specified product. But in analyzing economic development, it would be misleading to assume (as we do in the theory of the firm) that S_t consists only of the minimum cost techniques. Any student of economic development is well aware that institutional and socio-cultural considerations often lead communities to produce with economically non-optimal techniques. For any assumed ratio of factor prices, the techniques to produce a given amount of a particular product can be ranked in terms of descending cost, and an index function for the components of S_t can be derived.

of factors used in manufacturing a given output. But variations in S_t can modify income even if the total input of each factor is unaltered. For even with a fixed total employment of resources a reshuffling of the physical inputs among firms and industries can result in a greater over-all efficiency of production.

Our last variable, U_t, represents the entire social, cultural, and institutional complex of society.[9] From a purely economic point of view, U_t specifies the institutional "rules of the game," which must be observed in allocation and distribution. It tells us, for example, whether the economy is primarily competitive or monopolistic, capitalistic or socialistic, etc. Therefore, changes in U_t, like variations in S_t, can make independent contributions to total output even when the amounts of the physical inputs and the state of technology are held constant. As economists, of course, we have very little to say about many of U_t's components and about the determination of the rate of change of U_t through time. But the inclusion of this non-economic variable in our analysis is important for two reasons.

First, it constitutes an explicit recognition of the fact that long-term economic trends are not determined by purely economic factors. Therefore it enables the economist to talk about the impact of alterations in the underlying value systems of the society, changes in the mode of organization of the community, modifications of traditional institutions, etc., without artificially tacking them on as amendments to the body of analysis.

Second, our procedure may also show the non-economic social scientist who is interested in the explanation of economic phenomena how best to bring his specialized techniques to bear in analyzing the determinants of economic progress of different nations. Since this quantity U_t serves as a link between traditional economic thought, on the one hand, and sociology, social psychology, anthropology, political science, and history, on the other, the introduction of a socio-cultural variable into the framework of economic analysis will permit the social scientist to contribute more effectively to the understanding of economic phenomena. Note that U_t, too, is a vector, each of whose w components is an indicator of some economically relevant feature of the institutional or socio-cultural setup of the society in year t.

The argument so far may be summarized in the following proposition: the rate of the economy's output is a function not only of the employment level of capital, labor, and land, but also of the technology and skills used in production and of the socio-cultural environment in which the economy operates. If we now drop all the subscripts t, remembering that all the variables are functions of time, we may write the rate of growth of real income during a time interval Δt as

$$(2.2)\quad \frac{\Delta Y}{\Delta t} = \sum_{j=1}^{p} \frac{\Delta Y}{\Delta K_j}\frac{\Delta K_j}{\Delta t} + \sum_{j=1}^{q} \frac{\Delta Y}{\Delta N_j}\frac{\Delta N_j}{\Delta t} + \sum_{j=1}^{r} \frac{\Delta Y}{\Delta L_j}\frac{\Delta L_j}{\Delta t} + \sum_{j=1}^{v} \frac{\Delta Y}{\Delta S_j}\frac{\Delta S_j}{\Delta t} + \sum_{j=1}^{w} \frac{\Delta Y}{\Delta U_j}\frac{\Delta U_j}{\Delta t}.$$

This expression is obtained by differencing (2.1).* In this equation $\Delta Y/\Delta K_j$, $\Delta Y/\Delta N_j$, $\Delta Y/\Delta L_j$, $\Delta Y/\Delta S_j$, and $\Delta Y/\Delta U_j$ stand for the marginal physical products of the jth type of capital, land, labor, technology, and institutions, respectively, at a given point of time. The first three terms are familiar to the economist. They represent the increment to output due to an increased use of a specific kind of input, holding the amounts of all others fixed. The marginal product of technology, $\Delta Y/\Delta S_j$, is defined in an analogous manner. It is the difference between the total product of two equal bundles of capital, land, and labor obtained with a small variation in the jth technique of production under unchanging social and political environment. Just like the marginal products of the physical inputs, $\Delta Y/\Delta S_j$ will generally be non-negative (at least in a normal capitalist society) throughout the economically interesting range. For with respect to innovations we can assume the principle of "survival of the fittest": only those innovations which do not decrease total output will actually be adopted.

* Difference analysis is chosen over the differential approach in order not to limit the discussion to continuous variables and functions. This is particularly desirable when dealing with variables like S_t and U_t, which typically are subject to discrete shifts. Furthermore, one can evaluate $\Delta Y/\Delta S_j$ and $\Delta Y/\Delta U_j$ for particular, specific changes $\Delta S_j/\Delta t$ and $\Delta U_j/\Delta t$ even if S and U cannot be quantified. For example, the contribution to output of a change in the steel industry from technique x to technique y can be estimated even if we cannot write down a unique number for the corresponding $\Delta S_j/\Delta t$. Similarly, the effects upon production of a shift from a purely competitive system to a world of monopolies can be evaluated even without a measurement of the corresponding $\Delta U_j/\Delta t$.

Conceptually speaking, we may assign a meaning analogous to that of $\Delta Y/\Delta S_j$ to the marginal contribution of institutions, $\Delta Y/\Delta U_j$. In principle, $\Delta Y/\Delta U_j$ may be taken as a measure of the difference in the rate of output produced by a labor force of given size, working with the same technology and skills and using the same amounts of cooperating factors, but whose outlook, aspirations, and habits have been molded under slightly different social climates and by slightly different histories. Unlike $\Delta Y/\Delta S_j$, however, the marginal contribution of institutions may be either positive or negative. Generally speaking, the effectiveness of a given socio-cultural milieu in raising output is not the only criterion that determines the choice of institutional environment. In fact, legal, religious, and social patterns often persist long after they have outlived their economic usefulness. If

$$\sum_{j=1}^{w} \frac{\Delta Y}{\Delta U_j} \frac{\Delta U_j}{\Delta t}$$

is negative, changes in the socio-cultural milieu will be said to be growth-inhibiting; if this summation is positive, socio-cultural forces will be considered to be growth-promoting; and if it is zero, changes in institutional factors will be termed neutral with respect to economic progress.

If the shape of our production function $f(K, N, L, S, U)$ were given, the respective marginal productivities of capital, labor, land, techniques, and institutions would have known functional forms; i.e., given the form of equation (2.1), the marginal products $\Delta Y/\Delta K_j$, $\Delta Y/\Delta N_j$, $\Delta Y/\Delta L_j$, $\Delta Y/\Delta S_j$, $\Delta Y/\Delta U_j$ can be evaluated. But, as can be seen from (2.2), these data are insufficient to establish the rate of the economy's change of output, since $\Delta Y/\Delta t$ depends also upon the quantities $\Delta K_j/\Delta t$, $\Delta N_j/\Delta t$, $\Delta L_j/\Delta t$, $\Delta S_j/\Delta t$, and $\Delta U_j/\Delta t$. These represent, respectively, the rate of capital accumulation, the rate of change of natural resources, the rate of increase of the labor force, the rate of introduction of innovations, and the rate of change of the institutional index. In order to complete the system, then, we must specify a set of equations that will govern the time paths of each variable.

In the general case, the arguments of these new equations will include all the variables of the system. In addition, the variable time (t) may also enter explicitly into the equation, as it is possible that the *age* of the economy (however it may be measured) may have a direct bearing upon, say, the willingness of the community to engage in capital accumulation, the tendency to procreate, etc. A general form which our additional equations will take is as follows:

$$\Delta K_j/\Delta t = k(Y, K, N, L, S, U, t) \qquad j=1,\ldots,p. \tag{2.3}$$

$$\Delta N_j/\Delta t = n(Y, K, N, L, S, U, t) \qquad j=1,\ldots,q. \tag{2.4}$$

$$\Delta L_j/\Delta t = l(Y, K, N, L, S, U, t) \qquad j=1,\ldots,r. \tag{2.5}$$

$$\Delta S_j/\Delta t = s(Y, K, N, L, S, U, t) \qquad j=1,\ldots,v. \tag{2.6}$$

$$\Delta U_j/\Delta t = u(Y, K, N, L, S, U, t) \qquad j=1,\ldots,w. \tag{2.7}$$

These equations do not imply that the theories explaining the determination of, say, $\Delta K_j/\Delta t$, must be couched in terms of Y, K, N, L, S, U, and t. Subsidiary variables (such as the behavior of profit rates through time) can be introduced in order to explain these time paths. But, if we assume that the set of equations (2.1) and (2.3)–(2.7) constitute a complete system, the behavior through time of the subsidiary variables must be governed either by the time paths of some (or all) of the original variables of our system (i.e., by Y, K, N, L, S, and/or U), or else these paths must be determined exogenously. (In the latter cases, the time path of the subsidiary variable may be written as a function only of time.) Under these circumstances, one can modify the functional form of equations (2.3)–(2.7) so that only Y, K, N, L, S, U, and t appear as independent variables. That is, even when subsidiary explanatory variables are introduced into the analysis, the system may still be expressed in the form given for (2.3)–(2.7).

Let us examine each of these equations in turn. The capital accumulation equation (2.3) reflects, among other forces, such diverse factors as the society's propensity to save out of income, its willingness to invest and bear risk, the influence of credit institutions, the consequences of taxation, and the impact of changes in religious mores. Not all such effects appear explicitly in equation (2.3). The impact of the rate of inflation, for example, may show up in (2.3) through its relationship to the rate of growth of output $\Delta Y/\Delta t$; the rate of inflation will, therefore, serve to modify, among other quantities, the coefficients of powers of Y. Similarly, the influence of foreign loans and grants may be felt through the response of $\Delta K_j/\Delta t$ to K. In short, this equation is sufficiently general to include any force, economic or otherwise, that can affect the time path of the capital stock. The four remaining equations (2.4)–(2.7) obviously have the analogous property.

The resource change equation (2.4) reflects the influence of population pressure upon new resource discoveries (through the dependence upon L), the effect of technological change upon the resource levels in a country (through S), the impact of social and institutional forces upon the rate of resource exploitation (via U), the influence of the availability of capital equipment upon the rate of mining the natural wealth (by way of K), and the pressure of final demand upon resource use (by means of Y).

Similarly, the shape of the labor force equation (2.5) includes, among other things, the response of birth and death rates to changes in the level of income (through the dependence upon Y), to urbanization (through U), to improvements in health and sanitation (through S), to religious mores and habits (via U), to increases in over-all wealth (through K), etc. Furthermore, it also takes into account the work-leisure preference patterns of the community (via Y and U), the demographic composition of the labor force (through L), and the influence of changes in technology upon the employment of labor (through S).

Among other forces, the innovation equation (2.6) mirrors the impact upon entrepreneurial activity of the socio-cultural factors (via U), the influence of, say, natural resource exhaustion upon technological change (through N), the impact of the capital–labor and wage–interest ratios upon the type of technological change taking place in the economy (through K, L, and Y),* and the influence of the current level of technology and education upon the rate of innovation (through S). The impact of the advance of knowledge abroad upon $\Delta S_j/\Delta t$ may, incidentally, be reflected in our system through an exogenous shock.

The form of the equation governing the rate of social and cultural change, (2.7), however, cannot be specified without a complete theory of the historical process; in Marx's words, it is necessary to "lay bare the laws of motion of society"—a staggering requirement indeed. Some of the important influences upon the rate of social, cultural, and po-

* This factor may determine, for example, whether innovations are primarily capital-using or capital-displacing.

litical change may be the very complexity and tenacity of the institutions themselves (through U and $\Delta U_j/\Delta t$); the pressure of income levels in the society, especially when compared with aspirations (via Y and, perhaps, U); the influence of the web of productive relationships of the economy upon its mode of organization, its constitutional and legal system, and its cultural outlook (via S, broadly interpreted); and the influence of educational levels upon the feasible type of political system (again through S).

In the general case, then, our structure for the explanation of growth will consist of equations (2.1) and (2.3)–(2.7). [Equation (2.2), which determines $\Delta Y/\Delta t$, was obtained by differencing (2.1), and therefore is not an independent equation.] Given the analytical forms of (2.1) and (2.3)–(2.7), the rate of growth of the economy $\Delta Y/\Delta t$ can, in principle, be evaluated by solving these equations simultaneously. For we have a set of $p + q + r + v + w + 1$ equations in an equal number of economic unknowns, which must be solved to give Y and each component of the vectors $K, N, L, S,$ and U as functions of time. In practice, of course, the solution of a set of simultaneous difference equations is extremely difficult, unless the equations should reduce to a much simpler form. But if the work is carried out, one can write down an explicit solution for the dynamic behavior of the rate of output of the economy:

$$(2.8) \qquad Y = Y(K_0, N_0, L_0, S_0, U_0; t; \alpha_1, \ldots, \alpha_j, \ldots).$$

In this expression, K_0, N_0, L_0, S_0 represent the employment of capital, natural resources, labor, and technical skills, respectively, at time zero, while U_0 expresses the status of the institutional character of the economy at the start. These quantities may be called the initial conditions of the system. The initial value of output (Y_0) may be computed either from (2.1) or (2.8).

The α_j in (2.8) are the coefficients, exponents, etc., of the various combinations of functions of the initial conditions and time which can appear when (2.8) is written out explicitly. They may be derived directly from the coefficients of (2.1) and (2.3)–(2.7). We shall refer to the α_j as the structural parameters of the economy.*

* The parameters α_j may also be considered to be statistically distributed. See Trygve Haavelmo, *A Study in the Theory of Economic Evolution*, pp. 67 ff.

The initial conditions and the structural parameters together determine completely the economic evolution and the future economic history of a community in the absence of external disturbances.[10] That is, barring strong exogenous influences, dissimilarities in the standard of living and in the rates of progress of various economies are traceable to inter-country differences in the values of the initial conditions and the structural coefficients.

Before we discuss these sets of constraints in detail, however, it would be desirable to define more precisely what we mean by $t = 0$. The selection of a point of time at which t is set equal to zero presents much the same kind of problem that confronts the historian who must choose an appropriate starting date for historical analysis. Basically, for an approach of this nature to be valid, the results of the investigation must be independent of the choice of initial time. Generally, however, it is most convenient to date progress from an occurrence that marks a significant break from the past. The initial conditions of a system are then determined by the economic attributes of the region at $t = 0$, i.e., its capital endowment, natural wealth, size of the labor force, skills, and socio-cultural traits at the time the evolutionary process begins. Thus, they reflect whether, at the start of our economic history, the region is over- or underpopulated; whether it originally has a high level of skills and technology relative to other resources; whether it has a large capital–labor ratio; and whether it possesses a high level of indigenous culture, with an institutional complex favorable to economic development.

The role that initial conditions play in economic dynamics can best be appreciated by considering a special case. Let us look at two regions with identical structural parameters. Then, from a given historical date, they will develop according to the same system of equations (2.1) and (2.3)–(2.7). If, however, we assume that the values of K_0, N_0, L_0, S_0, and U_0 differ in the two countries, we may ask, "How will this difference influence the historical process in the two regions?"

To answer this question we shall have to digress for a moment. The entire class of dynamic solutions for Y can be subdivided into three general subsets: (1) solutions with no stationary value at the point of time under consideration; (2) those with a unique stationary value at that time; and (3) those with more than one stationary value at that time. By a stationary value of Y we mean a value such that all the first partial derivatives of Y with respect to the independent variables (excluding time) vanish. If all the partial time derivatives of Y also vanish, the economy has reached a stationary state. Otherwise, it is in a state of equilibrium growth. Since each stationary value represents a potential state of equilibrium, we have thus divided our solutions, at each point of time, into classes with zero, one, or several equilibrium positions.

An equilibrium position has another property: it can be stable, unstable, or neutral with respect to a small displacement. It is stable if any small disturbance generates forces tending to restore the system to its undisturbed position; it is unstable if there is even a single small disturbance that can give rise to forces tending to drive the system further from this equilibrium position; and it is neutral if a small displacement generates neither type of force. Dynamic equilibrium is analogous: a system is in dynamic equilibrium if, in the absence of external disturbances, it is in a state of equilibrium growth. The dynamic equilibrium is stable if any small displacement of the system from its equilibrium path generates forces tending to drive the system back to that path. Similar extensions can be made for the other cases.

The stability characteristics of the solution for Y are quite significant for dynamic analysis. For example, a system possessing a unique, stable dynamic equilibrium path will, sooner or later, converge to this path. In a system with multiple stable equilibria, on the other hand, the configuration at $t = 0$ will determine which equilibrium, if any, will be attained. Indeed, in this situation, a sufficiently large exogenous disturbance in the appropriate direction, if imposed upon a system in stable equilibrium, may change the equilibrium path to which the system converges, possibly driving it to an unstable position.

It is important to point out here that, except for the case of an economy with a unique, stable solution, differences in initial conditions affect the attributes of the ultimate stationary state toward which the economy tends. Furthermore, such differences may also determine the system's stability characteristics. Thus, two economies differing solely in their initial conditions may possess very different dynamic properties and may, therefore, exhibit very dissimilar historical behavior. Indeed, if we assume the existence of two types of stable dynamic paths for output, one of which implies a steady positive rate of growth of total output while the other implies a zero rate of growth, the initial conditions of the system will determine toward which of these time paths the economy will converge. In this case, differences in initial conditions alone will suffice to explain the observed discrepancies in the economic performance of developed and underdeveloped economies.

From an economic point of view it is not surprising that initial conditions have a strong influence upon development. Consider, for example, two economies with identical structural parameters. If one of them is underpopulated but endowed with great natural wealth, while the other is, say, resource-poor and heavily populated, economic evolution may well be different in the two systems. And even if capital accumulation, technological progress, etc., were to become parallel in the two economies, their ultimate standards of living would not, in general, follow the same equilibrium path.

Within our framework, incidentally, it is possible to treat an abrupt exogenous change in the variables of a system as a change in initial conditions. One merely makes the new origin of time the instant of modification and computes the appropriate set of initial conditions (which, of course, will be different from what one would get by starting the evolution in the unaltered system at that time). For example, we can visualize the dismantling of a factory by an occupying military force starting at 7 A.M. on May 12, 1945, as a change in the value of K_0 ; we keep N_0, L_0, U_0, and S_0 unchanged and start the dating from that time. Similarly, a sudden removal of restrictions upon immigration can be formalized as affecting L_0, and random or irregular shocks upon the economy can be incorporated in an analogous manner.

The meaning of the structural parameters is more familiar to the economist. These coefficients reflect, first of all, the relevant behavioral propensities of the community. In addition, they include the impact of natural and technological constraints upon the economic performance of the society. Finally, they mirror the influence of outside economies upon the economy of the region. Thus, the structural constants measure the quantitative response of the community to objective economic possibilities.[11] To the extent that they vary from system to system, therefore, they reflect dissimilarities in human behavior. These discrepancies in economic response could, in turn, be due to evolutionary processes which took place before $t = 0$; that is, they may be due to prior differences in the economic or social histories of the countries in question. It stands to reason that the stimuli to which the community has been exposed in the past may condition the type of response that economic (and other) stimuli elicit in the future. Consequently, the nature of the economic and physical surroundings in which the economy has previously operated may influence both the quantitative and the qualitative reactions of the community to new environmental facts. It is evident, then, that an attempt to explain the reasons for inter-regional dissimilarities in structural coefficients would require an integration of history, social psychology, anthropology, sociology, and political science with economics.

Even in the absence of disparities in initial conditions, differences in the magnitudes of the behavioristic parameters result, of course, in divergent paths of economic progress. The structural coefficients affect not only the levels attained by the variables in the stationary state, but also the stability properties of the dynamic solutions, the amplitudes of their cyclical fluctuations, and the uniqueness of their equilibrium solutions. In this connection, it should also be noted that even small differences in structural parameters can cause very large discrepancies in the long-term conditions of various economies. A simple example may serve to illustrate this point. One dollar invested at 3 per cent compounded annually becomes, after 500 years, more than 2½ million dollars. But, if instead the interest rate were 4 per cent, it would be worth more than 300 million dollars!

Thus we see that we can account for dissimilarities in economic histories and in the current economic performances of various social and political units with a single set of equations (2.1) and (2.3)–(2.7). For we can ascribe differences in standards of living to differences in initial conditions or in behavioral parameters without having to resort to a special theory for each type of economic system. Each set of conditions and parameters determines a particular path of expansion for the national product through time. To every combination of these constants corresponds an economy with a unique dynamic profile. In view of the very large number of *a priori* possibilities for combinations of initial conditions and parameters, then, there would appear to be no problem in accounting for growth and stagnation, affluence and poverty, with the same theoretical apparatus. Indeed, it is the very wealth of *a priori* possibilities that makes analysis difficult,[12] especially if we want the analysis to culminate in specific policy recommendations.

One of the tasks of the economic theorist, therefore, is to narrow down the field of inquiry. He may do this by inserting special assumptions, which are presumed to be of fairly widespread relevance, into our general framework. These assumptions, as will be seen below, are equivalent to specifying orders of magnitude and algebraic signs for some of the structural coefficients of equations (2.1) and (2.3)–(2.7). This procedure eliminates a number of combinations from economic consideration. In this way, a certain amount of simplicity may be achieved, albeit at the cost of universal relevance.

All the theories of growth and development put forth by the classical, Marxian, neo-classical, and Keynesian economists may be viewed as special cases of our structure. Differences among these theories arise because of dissimilarities in the postulates concerning the nature of the structural parameters of the system. Before turning to a detailed examination of the major theories of growth, therefore, it might prove useful to illustrate briefly how differences in assumptions about the determinants of long-term economic trends may be translated into postulates about structural coefficients.

For example, some economists consider socio-cultural forces to be of great importance in conditioning the rate of progress of an economy; for these economists,

$$\sum_{j=1}^{w} \frac{\Delta Y}{\Delta U_j} \frac{\Delta U_j}{\Delta t}$$

is very large. Others consider socio-cultural influence to be negligible; for them, the absolute magnitude of this sum is quite small. This latter group will, in fact, generally omit socio-cultural factors from consideration altogether. Thus, the adherents of this school of thought will rewrite (2.1) without reference to U and will drop equation (2.7) from the system, since to them it is irrelevant to their analysis. Similarly, some authors, in discussing underdeveloped areas, restrict their comments to economies in which per capita output does not increase as population grows. The insertion of such special postulates into the general framework thus can be made to narrow the range of *a priori* possibilities considerably. In this manner, the analysis is made more tractable and the conclusions become testable.

In the following chapters our primary focus will be upon the treatment of the determinants of growth and stagnation by some of the great economists of the past. To simplify our exposition of their theories we shall treat $K, N, L, S,$ and U as single numbers (rather than as vectors) and assume that their production functions are differentiable. We shall ask several questions: How were differences in the long-term economic trends of various communities accounted for? What were believed to be the crucial growth-promoting and growth-inhibiting forces in the economy? And, most important, to what extent is the analysis pertinent to the contemporary problem of underdevelopment of major segments of our world?

We shall consider the answers to these questions given by Smith, Ricardo, Marx, and Schumpeter, and by the moderns. We shall emphasize how the doctrines of each of these economists fit into our general framework for analyzing growth, in the hope that the source of the differences in their conclusions will become clearer and that the unifying strands in their analyses will stand out. In this process, to the extent that the theories of all these authors may be formulated as special cases of our structure for growth we shall also have presented evidence for its general applicability.

THREE

ADAM SMITH

THE MAIN PROBLEM to which Adam Smith addressed himself is well summarized in the title of his book: *An Inquiry into the Nature and Causes of the Wealth of Nations.* Although his theory of value and distribution has received relatively more attention in the history of economic doctrine, his primary concern was evidently with the dynamic question of growth and development. He attempted to determine what factors were responsible for economic progress and what policy measures could be undertaken to create an environment favorable to rapid growth.

While his analysis is not so refined as that of his successors, he does offer an internally consistent dynamic model. The main strands of his theory—the investigation of capital accumulation, population growth, and labor productivity—still underlie all current treatments of the problem. And many of his policy recommendations, such as his plea in favor of free trade and his stand against planned economic development, are still as controversial now as when they were first made. A detailed study of his model may, therefore, prove to be of great interest.

THE PRODUCTION FUNCTION

Despite the fact that he considered labor to be the sole standard of value, Adam Smith recognized the existence of three factors of production: labor, capital (or "stock," as he called it), and land. Thus he wrote: "To him [the farmer], land is the only instrument which enables him to earn the wages of his labour, and to make the profits of this stock."[1] And again: "Wages, profit and rent, are the three original sources of all revenue as well as of all exchangeable value."[2] In our notation, his production function may therefore be expressed as

$$Y = f(K, L, N) . \tag{3.1}$$

This production function is not subject to the restriction of diminishing marginal productivity, inasmuch as he does not appear to have made this postulate. It is, however, subject to increasing returns to scale. Smith argued[3] that the real cost of production will tend to diminish with the passage of time as a result of the existence of internal and external economies arising from increases in market size. Economies of scale will be realized in production and in marketing owing to a greater degree of division of labor and to general improvements in machinery. Therefore, once set in motion, the development process will tend to be self-reinforcing.

Adam Smith also introduced another explicit assumption concerning the determinants of the productivity of labor and land. He attributed international and intertemporal variations in productivity to differences in the degree of division of labor. In a justly famous passage, he explained,

> This great increase of the quantity of work, which, in consequence of the division of labour, the same number of people are capable of performing, is owing to three different circumstances; first, to the increase of dexterity in every particular workman; secondly, to the saving of the time which is commonly lost in passing from one species of work to another; and lastly, to the invention of a great number of machines which facilitate and abridge labour, and enable one man to do the work of many.[4]

But the extent of the division of labor which can take place at any point of time depends on the size of the market:

> When the market is very small, no person can have any encouragement to dedicate himself entirely to one employment, for want of power to exchange all that surplus part of the produce of his own labour, which is over and above his own consumption, for such parts of the produce of other men's labour as he has occasion for.[5]

As a result, while the division of labor is technically feasible, its economic usefulness is limited by the extent of the market. And the size of the market is, in turn, a function of the amount of capital in existence,[6] and of the institutional restrictions that are placed upon trade.[7]

Thus, Smith argued: "As the accumulation of stock must, in the nature of things, be previous to the division of labour, so labour can be more and more subdivided in proportion only as stock is previously more and more accumulated."[8] A greater degree of division of labor may be achieved only if the same work force is provided with more tools and machinery with which to carry on production. Capital must therefore increase before further specialization takes place.

Furthermore, the size of the market and the productivity of labor are also influenced by the regulation of domestic and international trade. Any restriction upon free international commerce will of necessity limit the size of the market. And, by impeding international specialization of labor, trade restrictions will also lower domestic productivity.

> No regulation of commerce can increase the quantity of industry in any society beyond what its capital can maintain. It can only divert a part of it into a direction into which it might not otherwise have gone; and it is by no means certain that this artificial direction is likely to be more advantageous to the society than that into which it would have gone of its own accord.[9]

In view of these arguments, we may add two further restrictions to our specifications of the Smithian production function:

$$\frac{\partial f}{\partial L} = g(K, U)\,, \tag{3.2}$$

and

$$\frac{\partial f}{\partial K} = h(K, U)\,. \tag{3.3}$$

These restrictions state, respectively, that the marginal productivity of labor and of land are functionally related to the amounts of capital employed and to the institutional framework of the economy.

But what about the impact of changes in techniques upon productivity? Smith did not ignore this factor. He simply assumed that there is an automatic flow of innovations that allows the degree of division of labor to adjust itself to the size of the capital stock. Changes in productivity are therefore never impeded by lack of appropriate technological knowledge. Conversely, technological improvements can only be introduced to the extent that there is sufficient capital available.

> The person who employs his stock in maintaining labour, endeavours, therefore, both to make among his workmen the most proper distribution of employment, and to furnish them with the best machines which he can either invent or afford to purchase. His abilities in both these respects are generally in proportion to the extent of his stock, or to the number of people whom it can employ.[10]

The fund of knowledge need therefore not appear as an independent variable in (3.2) and (3.3).*

The growth rate of the annual flow of output of the economy may be obtained by differentiating (3.1). This results in

$$\frac{dY}{dt} = \frac{\partial f}{\partial L}\frac{dL}{dt} + \frac{\partial f}{\partial K}\frac{dK}{dt} + \frac{\partial f}{\partial N}\frac{dN}{dt}. \tag{3.4}$$

If we also substitute the restrictions (3.2) and (3.3) into (3.4), we get

$$\frac{dY}{dt} = g(K, U)\frac{dL}{dt} + \frac{\partial f}{\partial K}\frac{dK}{dt} + h(K, U)\frac{dN}{dt}. \tag{3.5}$$

To close the system, then, we must examine Smith's views on the determinants of the growth of employment of labor dL/dt, on the increase of land dN/dt, on capital accumulation dK/dt, and on the change in institutions dU/dt. If the form of (3.1) is given, $\partial f/\partial K$ can be evaluated and is not an independent quantity.

NATURAL RESOURCES AND INSTITUTIONS

Two of these factors may be dismissed quite rapidly: the rate of change of institutions and the increment per unit time of land. Smith considered dU/dt to be given exogenously; i.e., he thought its time path could be fixed arbitrarily, without regard to the rest of the variables in the system. To Smith the institutional variable is an important policy variable. Indeed, much of the burden of his argument in favor of free trade and *laissez faire* is designed to show how the institutional environment might best be altered in order to maximize the economy's rate of growth. Although we shall return to this question in greater detail when we discuss the policy implications of Adam Smith's theory, we may at this point merely state that

$$U = \overline{U}(t), \tag{3.6}$$

where $\overline{U}(t)$ is an exogenously fixed quantity.

With respect to land, Smith never explicitly stated that land was

* Alternatively, we may introduce S temporarily into (2.2) and (2.3) and then eliminate it with the aid of the postulate (2.3) $S = sK$, where s is a constant.

limited in supply. He may however have implied this postulate when he wrote: "The rent of land, therefore, considered as the price paid for the use of land, is naturally a monopoly price."[11] We therefore interpret Smith to say that land is fixed in quantity; i.e.,

$$\frac{dN}{dt} = 0\,. \tag{3.7}$$

This assumption may be used together with (3.3) to simplify the expression (3.5) for the economy's rate of growth. By substitution, we get the much simpler relationship

$$\frac{dY}{dt} = \frac{\partial f}{\partial K}\frac{dK}{dt} + g[K, \overline{U}(t)]\frac{dL}{dt}\,. \tag{3.8}$$

In the above expression there are only two independent variables, dL/dt and dK/dt (K is completely defined by dK/dt and the initial stock of capital). The determinants of the time paths of these two variables must be analyzed before we are in a position to understand Smith's theory of economic development.

THE LABOR FORCE

The growth of the labor force is related, on the supply side, to population. In the long run, according to Smith, population growth is regulated by the funds available for human sustenance. "Every species of animals naturally multiplies in proportion to the means of their subsistence and no species can ever multiply beyond it."[12] Consequently, the wage rate plays a crucial role in determining population size. When wages are high, early marriages are encouraged, and birth rates tend to rise. A more liberal reward of labor also enables the rearing of more children to maturity. The consequent decline in infant mortality, coupled with the rise in birth rates, implies a more rapid rate of population growth. On the other hand, when wage rates are low, the process is reversed. High infant mortality and postponement of marriage slow down the tempo of population expansion.

The limiting wage rate is that which is neither sufficiently high to permit an increase in numbers nor sufficiently low to force a shrinkage of the population base. Smith called this rate the "subsistence wage," one which is consistent with a constant population.

Smith's population theory may be summarized in the following statement: the rate of population growth (and, therefore, the rate of expansion of the supply of labor, which we shall designate by the symbol dL_S/dt) varies as the difference between the actual money wage rate (w) and the subsistence wage ($\bar{w}$). If actual wages exceed the level of subsistence, population will increase; if actual wages are below subsistence, population will decline; and if market wages equal the subsistence wage, population will be constant. Mathematically, this statement may be expressed as

$$\frac{dL_S}{dt} = q(w - \bar{w}) \,, \tag{3.9}$$

where $q > 0$. On the average, the supply of labor is "as nearly as possible in the proportion which the demand for labour requires," and therefore, in the long run,

$$\frac{dL_S}{dt} = \frac{dL_D}{dt} \,, \tag{3.10}$$

where dL_D/dt stands for changes in the demand for labor. "If this demand is continually increasing, the reward of labour must necessarily encourage in such a manner the marriage and multiplication of labourers, as may enable them to supply the continually increasing demand by a continually increasing population." In a purely competitive labor market, if the wage rate falls temporarily below what is necessary to maintain the demand and supply of labor in balance, the pressure of demand will act to raise it. Conversely, should wages be above the equilibrium level, then the excess supply resulting from too rapid a growth of population will soon lower the remuneration of labor. "It is in this manner that the demand for men, like that for any other commodity, necessarily regulates the production of men; quickens it when it goes too slowly, and stops it when it advances too fast."

But what determines the demand for labor? Smith's answer is that

> The demand for those who live by wages, it is evident, cannot increase but in proportion to the increase of the funds which are destined for the payment of wages. These funds are of two kinds: first, the revenue which is over and above what is necessary for the maintenance; and, secondly, the stock which is over and above what is necessary for the employment of their masters.[18]

This is the wages-fund doctrine. It relates the employment of labor to the size of the revolving fund destined for the maintenance of the labor force.

> The demand for those who live by wages, therefore, necessarily increases with the increase of the revenue and stock of every country, and cannot possibly increase without it. The increase of revenue and stock is the increase in national wealth. The demand for those who live by wages, therefore, naturally increases with the increase of national wealth, and cannot possibly increase without it.[14]

This dependence of changes in the demand for labor upon the wages fund may be expressed as

$$\frac{dL_D}{dt} = a\,\frac{dK}{dt} + b\,\frac{dY}{dt}, \tag{3.11}$$

where a and b are positive factors of proportionality. Putting (3.9), (3.10), and (3.11) together, we may summarize Smith's theory of the labor market in the following two propositions:

$$\frac{dL}{dt} = a\,\frac{dK}{dt} + b\,\frac{dY}{dt}, \tag{3.12}$$

and

$$(w - \bar{w}) = \frac{a}{q} \cdot \frac{dK}{dt} + \frac{b}{q} \cdot \frac{dY}{dt}. \tag{3.13}$$

The first statement relates the growth of the labor force to the growth of income and capital. It implies that in an expanding economy population will be growing, that in a retrogressing economy it will be declining, and that in the stationary state it will be constant.

The second expression tells us something concerning the course of the wage rate: High wage rates exist in growing economies, low wage rates in declining ones; and the level of subsistence is characteristic of the stationary state. Thus, "It is not the actual greatness of national wealth, but its continual increase, which occasions a rise in the wages of labour. It is not, accordingly, in the richest countries, but in the most thriving or in those which are growing rich the fastest, that the wages of labour are highest,"[15] because the supply of labor is continually trying to catch up with demand.

If, then, in the previous period demand was high, the labor force will have expanded sufficiently to match this demand. Unless the current period witnesses another rise in demand, wages will fall to subsistence. They cannot remain above subsistence in the absence of a new increase in demand, because higher than subsistence wages will spur population growth. This will give rise to excess supply in the labor market, which, under purely competitive conditions, will drive wage rates down. Hence,

> It deserves to be remarked, perhaps, that it is in the progressive state, while the society is advancing to the further acquisition, rather than when it has acquired its full complement of riches, that the condition of the labouring poor, of the great body of the people, seems to be happiest and the most comfortable. It is hard in the stationary, and miserable in the declining state. The progressive state is in reality the cheerful and the hearty state to all the different orders of society. The stationary is dull, the declining is melancholy.[16]

Let us now substitute the labor-growth equation (3.12) into the expression that describes the rate of change of the national product (3.8). This procedure yields

$$(3.14)\qquad \frac{dY}{dt} = \frac{\partial f}{\partial K}\frac{dK}{dt} + g[K, \overline{U}(t)]\left(a\frac{dK}{dt} + b\frac{dY}{dt}\right).$$

If we collect the terms in dY/dt on the left-hand side of the equation we get

$$(3.15)\qquad \frac{dY}{dt}\{1 - bg[K, \overline{U}(t)]\} = \frac{dK}{dt}\left\{\frac{\partial f}{\partial K} + ag[K,\overline{U}(t)]\right\},$$

or

$$(3.16)\qquad \frac{dY}{dt} = \frac{dK}{dt}\,\frac{(\partial f/\partial K) + ag[K, \overline{U}(t)]}{1 - bg[K, \overline{U}(t)]}.$$

This form of the income-growth equation emphasizes the cardinal importance of capital accumulation to the growth process. In Smith's analysis, the rate of output expansion goes hand in hand with the rate of investment. It is only when investment is positive that output expands. A constant capital stock, no matter how high, implies stagnation. A declining capital stock implies retrogression. Furthermore, the size of the economy's capital stock also determines the magnitude of the factor of proportionality between dY/dt and dK/dt. The higher K is, the larger the numerator of (3.16) and the smaller the denominator will be. In a growing economy, therefore, in which K is expanding, a given increment in capital will lead to a higher absolute increase in the level of output as time goes on.

The explanation of this phenomenon lies in the fact that a greater capital stock results in more division of labor, which raises the productivity of labor. As a result, the marginal capital–output ratio $(dK/dt)/(dY/dt)$ falls. As long as capital accumulation continues at the same rate, then, economic development will be cumulative, unless adverse exogenous changes in $\overrightarrow{U}(t)$ take place. It should also be noted that detrimental institutional developments can decrease markedly the impact of capital accumulation upon the economy's rate of growth. By the same token, favorable political and socio-cultural forces can serve to enhance the growth-promoting impact of investment.

THE ACCUMULATION OF CAPITAL

In view of the crucial role played by capital accumulation in Adam Smith's system, we must ask: "How is the rate of investment determined?" Smith would answer: "By the rate of saving." In fact, he wrote, "Capitals are increased by parsimony and diminished by prodigality and misconduct."[17] Obviously, he did not admit the possibility of leakages occurring between the flow of saving and the transformation of this flow into investment, since according to his argument:

> Whatever a person saves from his revenue he adds to his capital, and either employs it himself in maintaining an additional number of productive hands, or enables some other person to do so, by lending it to him for an interest, that is, for a share of profits. As the capital of an individual can be increased only by what he saves from his annual revenue or his annual gains, so the capital of society, which is the same with that of all the individuals who compose it, can be increased only in the same manner.

And again: "That portion which he (a rich man) annually saves . . . for the sake of profit . . . is immediately employed as a capital." And more strongly still,

> In all countries where there is tolerable security, every man of common understanding will endeavour to employ whatever stock he can command, in procuring either present employment or future profit. If it is employed in procuring present employment, it is a stock reserved for immediate consumption. If it is employed in procuring future profit, it must procure this profit either by staying with him, or by going from him. In the one case it is fixed, in the other circulating capital. *A man must be perfectly crazy* who, where there is tolerable security, does not employ all the stock which he commands, whether it be his own or borrowed of other people, in some one or other of those three ways.[18]

But what governs the allocation of income as between consumption and saving (or investment)? Smith asserts that the "consideration of his own private profit, is the sole motive which determines the owner of any capital to employ it."[19] And, since Smith identifies savings with investment, the implication is that profits also supply the motive for saving. The ability to save and invest is, however, limited by income.

> The capital of all individuals of a nation is increased in the same manner as that of a single individual, by their continually accumulating and adding whatever they save out of their income. It is likely to increase the fastest, therefore, when it is employed in the way that affords the greatest revenue to all the inhabitants of the country, as they will thus be enabled to make the greatest savings.[20]

The desire to save and invest for profit is a normal one: "As soon as stock has accumulated in the hands of particular persons, some of them will *naturally* employ it in setting to work industrious people."[21] For "Every individual is continually exerting himself to find the most advantageous employment for whatever capital he commands."[22] As a result, as long as there are any profits over and above compensation for risk to be made by investment, capital accumulation will continue. Provisionally, therefore, we may state that

$$\frac{dK}{dt} = k(r - \bar{r}, Y)\,, \tag{3.17}$$

where $\partial k/\partial Y > 0$, r stands for the rate of profits at time t, and $\bar{r}$ denotes its minimum value. It should be noted that the time path of

$(r - \bar{r})$ and the manner of the dependence of capital accumulation upon this quantity have, as yet, been left unspecified.

In the course of economic progress, as the economy's capital stock grows, the rate of profits will generally fall. "As riches, improvement and population have increased, interest has declined."[23] Smith's reason for this is, however, somewhat unconvincing: It lies in the competition of capitalists. "When the stock of many rich merchants are turned into the same trade, their mutual competition naturally tends to lower its profit; and when there is a like increase of stock in all the different trades carried on in the same society, the same competition must produce the same effect on them all."[24] As a result of the growth of the economy's capital stock, the wage rate will be bid up as entrepreneurs compete against each other for scarce labor.[25] Also, the more profitable investment opportunities will be taken first. A larger capital stock can therefore be employed only at a lower (marginal) profit ratio. Implied here is a negatively sloping marginal efficiency of capital curve. Although Smith postulated that the marginal productivity of labor increases with the amount of capital used, he gives no good reason that this should, in fact, be the case. In any event, he assumed that the "increase of stock, which raises wages, tends to lower profit."[26]

Another important influence upon the rate of profit is the institutional environment—the degree of regulation of commerce, the degree of monopoly or competition, and the control of international trade.[27] With respect to these matters, Smith argued that the interest of profit receivers does not always coincide with that of society.*

Finally, the actual rate of profit also includes a risk premium.[28] The minimum rate of profit $(\bar{r})$ is sufficient to compensate for this factor.[29] The height of the risk premium is also strongly affected by the institutional structure. Smith cites as being important here the security of property and the legality of lending operations.[30] His theory of profit may therefore be summarized in the following statement:

$$r - \bar{r} = m[K, \overline{U}(t)]\,, \tag{3.18}$$

where $\partial m/\partial K < 0$.

---

* One wonders, however, whether at this point he did not confuse the goal of profit rate maximization with that of maximizing total profits. See Smith, *The Wealth of Nations,* p. 250.

How will this secular decline in interest rates affect capital accumulation? Smith considered the supply curve of capital as a function of the interest rate to be negatively sloped. He argued that when the *rentiers*—who live on income from lending—are faced with a drop in interest rates, they will actually increase (rather than decrease) their lending activity in order to maintain a certain standard of living. If the interest rate is high, the only borrowers who can afford to pay are "prodigals and projectors"; only a small amount will therefore be lent. With a reduction in interest rates entrepreneurs will enter the loanable funds market. "A great part of the capital of the country is thus thrown into the hands in which it is most likely to be employed with advantage."[31] But at these lower interest rates more must be lent to obtain the same income.

As the interest rate drops still further, *rentiers* will find that they can no longer live on property income: they will then be forced to turn entrepreneurs themselves.

> As the ordinary rate of clear profit would be very small, so the usual market rate of interest which could be afforded out of it, would be so low as to render it impossible for any but the very wealthiest of people to live upon the interest of their money. All people of small or middling fortunes would be obliged to superintend themselves the employment of their own stocks. It would be necessary that almost every man should be a man of business, or engage in some sort of trade. The province of Holland seems to be approaching near to this state. It is there unfashionable not to be a man of business.[32]

By means of social changes such as these, capital accumulation will continue despite the low rate of interest. In fact, according to Smith: "It is with industrious nations, who are advancing in the acquisition of riches, as with industrious individuals. A great stock, though with small profits, generally increases faster than a small stock with greater profits."[33] This happy state of affairs will continue until the country has acquired "that full complement of riches which the nature of its soil and climate, and its situation with respect to other countries, allowed it to acquire." When the country possesses as much capital as it can profitably employ, and is "fully stocked in proportion to all the business it had to transact," the rate of interest will drop to $\bar{r}$. No more profits, net of risk, can be made from further investment. Capital accumulation will then stop. Population will remain constant. The economy will have reached the stationary state.

THE TIME PATH OF THE ECONOMY

We are now in a position to trace out the dynamic process as visualized by Adam Smith. By substituting (3.18) into (3.17), we get

$$\frac{dK}{dt} = k\{m[K, \overline{U}(t)], Y\}. \tag{3.19}$$

In a progressive economy both dY/dt and dK/dt are positive. The growing level of income will tend to increase the rate of capital accumulation, since $\partial k/\partial Y$ is also positive. Furthermore, an increasing capital stock will also tend to enhance the rate of capital formation. The larger capital stock will tend to depress the rate of profits on investment, whereas the fall in interest rate will tend to *increase* the rate of capital expansion (provided, of course, that r still exceeds $\bar{r}$).* As a result of this, in a growing economy, capital will go up by larger and larger increments in each succeeding period.

But we have also seen from equation (3.16) that with economic development the incremental capital–output ratio falls through time. This is due to the influence of capital upon the productivity of labor. Therefore, the larger values of dK/dt will result in even greater increases in the economy's rate of output dY/dt. Economic development will consequently be a cumulative process. It will proceed at an accelerated pace, until the economy's capital stock is so large that the rate of profits drops to $\bar{r}$. Then the economy will have attained "its full complement of riches," and the stationary state sets in. This process is portrayed graphically in Fig 3.1.†

---

* This is merely a verbal expression of the chain rule

$$\frac{\partial k}{\partial K} = \frac{\partial k}{\partial m}\frac{\partial m}{\partial K};$$

since $\partial k/\partial m < 0$ and $\partial m/\partial K < 0$, $\partial k/\partial K > 0$.

† The time rate of income in Fig. 3.1 has an **S**-shape because the supply price of risk capital, $\bar{r}$, differs for different individuals. Hence the approach to the stationary state will be gradual.

Smith's example of an expanding economy was North America. He wrote:

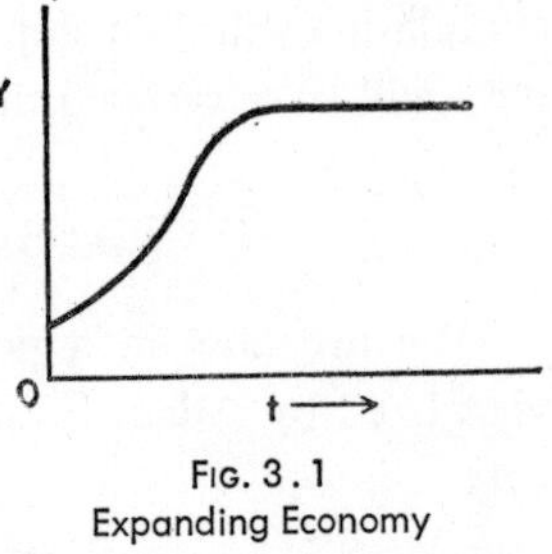

FIG. 3.1
Expanding Economy

> But though North America is not yet as rich as England, it is much more thriving, and advancing with much greater rapidity to the further acquisition of riches. . . . Labour is there so well rewarded that a numerous family of children, instead of being a burden is a source of opulence and prosperity to the parents. . . . The demand for labourers, the funds destined to maintain them, increase it seems, still faster than they can find labourers to employ.
>
> . . .
>
> In our North American and West Indian colonies, not only the wages of labour, but the interest of money, and consequently the profits of stock, are higher than in England. . . . A new colony must always for some time be more under-stocked in proportion to the extent of its territory, and more under-peopled in proportion to the extent of its stock, than the greater part of other countries. They have more land than they have stock to cultivate. . . . Stock employed in the purchase and improvement of such lands must yield a very large profit, and consequently afford to pay a very large interest. Its rapid accumulation in so profitable an employment enables the planter to increase the number of his hands faster than he can find them in a new settlement. Those whom he can find, therefore, are very liberally rewarded. As the colony increases, the profits of stock gradually diminish. . . . As riches, improvement and population have increased, interest has declined. The wages of labour do not sink with the profit of stock. The demand for labour increases with the increase of stock whatever be its profits; and after these are diminished, stock may not only continue to increase, but to increase much faster than before.[34]

No wonder, then, that Adam Smith identified the progressive economy with the "cheerful and hearty state"!

The opposite situation obtains in countries that are retrogressing. Bengal provided Smith with an example of such a state.[35] In antiquity, Bengal had had a flourishing economy, whose wealth was based primarily upon inland trade on navigable waters. By Smith's time, however, her population and her wealth had been "sensibly decaying";[36] profits were still very high.[37] However, instead of accelerating the rate of capital formation, the high rates of profit enabled the *rentiers* to derive sufficient incomes from only a small amount of capital; the capitalists, therefore, devoted part of their accumulated stock to conspicuous consumption. The decline in capital led to a fall in the demand for labor; wages fell below subsistence; as a result, "want, famine, and mortality" were familiar features of the economic landscape, and population was fast shrinking. Furthermore, the very decline of the economy's capital stock led to a still further rise in profits, drop in wages, decline in population. . . . The cumulative process downward, once started, became self-reinforcing.

We have, then, in Adam Smith's analysis, a description of an unstable dynamic process. Starting from an equilibrium situation, any upward displacement leads to further upward movement; and any movement downward likewise becomes cumulative in nature. Are there any limits to these cumulative processes?

According to Smith, the natural upper limit is the stationary state. Growth cannot persist forever. Eventually, as a result of sustained capital accumulation, the rate of profits must fall to $\bar{r}$. The economy will then enter the stationary state. Smith described this condition as follows:

> In a country which had acquired that full complement of riches which the nature of its soil and climate, and its situation with respect to other countries, allowed it to acquire; which could, therefore, advance no further, and which was not going backwards, both the wages of labour and the profits of stock would probably be very low. In a country fully peopled in proportion to what either its territory could maintain or its stock employ, the competition for employment would necessarily be so great as to reduce the wages of labour to what was barely sufficient to keep up the number of labourers, and, the country being already fully peopled, that number could never be augmented. In a country fully stocked in proportion to all the business it had to transact, as great a quantity of stock would be employed in every particular branch as the nature and extent of trade would admit. The competition, therefore, would everywhere be as great, and consequently the ordinary profit as low as possible.[38]

The stationary state, is not, however, a state of underdevelopment. True, there is no growth in such a community; per capita output is stagnant, wages are at the subsistence level, profits are at the minimum consistent with risk, no net investment takes place, population remains unchanged, and total income is constant. However, in this case nothing can be done to remedy this "dull" state of affairs. The economy has in fact reached the maximum degree of opulence consistent with its natural environment. By our definition, then, it is not underdeveloped. A truly underdeveloped community, according to Smith, is China,[39] which is a case of an economy stagnant *before* it has reached the maximum degree of riches attainable with its natural resources.

We have seen, then, that for Adam Smith, the evolution of the economy can follow many different routes. Growth or retrogression, stationary state or underdevelopment—what determines which of these time paths and states the economy will choose? This is the crux of the matter. We may arrive at the answer in several different ways. If we knew the analytical form of the capital accumulation equation (3.19) and of the income-growth relationship (3.14), we could solve them simultaneously. The resulting solution for the economy's rate of output would have the general form

$$Y = y[K_0, L_0, N_0; \alpha_1, \ldots, \alpha_N; \overline{U}(t)]. \tag{3.20}$$

Thus, the dynamic progress of the economy is seen to depend upon the initial conditions (K_0, N_0, L_0) and upon the structural parameters ($\alpha_1, \ldots, \alpha_N$) as before. But it also depends upon the exogenously determined historical change in the institutional environment [$U(t)$]. Since Smith took the initial conditions and the behavioral propensities to be given for the problem, he argued that the reason for growth or stagnation is to be found in the nature of the institutional setting. A poor legal system was responsible for the situation of China in Smith's time; adverse economic and political institutions must be blamed for Bengal's plight. Smith argued:

> China seems to have been long stationary, and had probably long ago acquired that full complement of riches which is consistent with the nature of its laws and institutions. But this complement may be much inferior to what, with other laws and institutions, the nature of its soil, climate, and situation might admit of.[40]

In the case of Bengal, he wrote: "The difference between the genius of the British constitution which protects and governs North America, and that of the mercantile company which oppresses and domineers in the East Indies, cannot perhaps be better illustrated than by the different state of those countries."[41]

To summarize Adam Smith's argument, the fundamental economic determinant of growth is the rate of capital formation. In fact, as is apparent from equation (3.16), the rate of progress of the economy is actually proportional to its rate of investment.

> The annual produce of the land and labour of any nation can be increased in its value by no other means but by increasing either the number of its productive labourers, or the productive powers of those labourers who had before been employed. The number of its productive labourers, it is evident, can never be much increased, but in consequence of an increase of capital, or of the funds destined for maintaining them. The productive powers of the same number of labourers cannot be increased, but in consequence either of some addition and improvement to those machines and instruments which facilitate and abridge labour; or of a more proper division and distribution of employment. In either case an additional capital is almost always required. . . . When we compare, therefore, the state of a nation at two different periods, and find, that the annual produce of its land and labour is evidently greater at the latter than the former, that its lands are better cultivated, its manufactures more extensive, we may be assured that its capital must have increased during the interval between those two periods.[42]

However, the rate of capital formation depends crucially upon the relationship between the market rate of net profits (r) and the minimum consistent with compensation for risk bearing ($\bar{r}$). Both of these quantities are dependent upon the institutional setup. Freedom of international trade, regulation of competition, security of life and property, political institutions, all play a role in establishing the relationship between r and $\bar{r}$. By closing the gap between r and $\bar{r}$, adverse legislation can choke off all capital formation. A favorable political and legal environment, on the other hand, can contribute significantly toward increasing the flow of investment.

Institutions, then, are Adam Smith's answer to the problem of economic development. Specifically, he was a staunch advocate of free trade,[43] as it insured domestic productivity by widening the extent of the market. Furthermore, by permitting international division of labor, free trade also contributed toward raising the output of the world as a whole. Domestically, Smith favored a policy of nonintervention. In a well-known passage, he argued:

> But the annual revenue of every society is always precisely equal to the exchangeable value of the whole produce of its industry, or rather is precisely the same thing with that exchangeable value. As every individual, therefore, endeavours as much as he can both to employ his capital in the support of domestic industry, and so to direct that industry that its produce be of the greatest value; every individual necessarily labours to render the annual revenue of society as great as he can . . . he intends only his own gain, and he is in this, as in many other cases, led by an invisible hand to promote an end which was no part of his intention.

Therefore:

> The statesman, who should attempt to direct private people in what manner they ought to employ their capitals, would not only load himself with a most unnecessary attention, but assume an authority which could safely be trusted, not only to no single person, but to no council or senate whatever, and which would nowhere be so dangerous as in the hands of a man who had the folly and presumption enough to fancy himself fit to exercise it.[44]

Evidently, Adam Smith left no room for doubt about where he stood on the modern question of planning for economic development.

FOUR

RICARDO

THE PRODUCTION FUNCTION

DAVID RICARDO's production function, like Adam Smith's, postulates the existence of three factors—land, labor, and capital. In contrast to Smith's function, however, Ricardo's is subject to diminishing marginal productivity,[1] which stems from the fact that land is variable in quality and fixed in supply. As a result, the marginal productivity not only of land itself but also of capital and labor declines as cultivation is increased. In response to increasing population pressures, the margin of cultivation may have to be extended to less fertile land. Under these circumstances, the same doses of capital and labor applied to the less "productive" land would yield a smaller increment of produce. This case, which is known in post-Ricardian literature as the case of the extensive margin, was described by Ricardo in the following manner:

> Thus suppose land—No. 1, 2, 3—to yield, with an equal employment of capital and labour, a net produce of 100, 90, and 80 quarters of corn.* In a new country, where there is an abundance of fertile land compared with the population, and where therefore it is only necessary to cultivate No. 1, the whole net produce will belong to the cultivator, and will be the profits of stock which he advances. As soon as population has so far increased as to make it necessary to cultivate No. 2, increased rent would commence on No. 1.[2]

On the other hand, assume that the area previously under cultivation is subjected to more intensive agricultural exploitation: as larger doses of capital and labor are applied to the same amount of land, successively smaller increments in output will result; and hence, the factors of production are no longer combined in a strictly optimal fashion.

* A quarter is 8 bushels, or approximately a quarter of a ton.

This alternative has been labeled the case of the intensive margin, and Ricardo wrote of it as follows:

> It often, and indeed, commonly happens, that before No. 2, 3, 4, or 5, or the inferior lands are cultivated, capital can be employed more productively on those lands which are already in cultivation. It may perhaps be found that by doubling the original capital employed on No. 1, though the produce will not be doubled, will not be increased by 100 quarters, it may be increased by eighty-five quarters, and that this quantity exceeds what would be obtained by employing the same capital on land No. 3.[3]

Regardless of which course of action is followed, however, the marginal productivity of land, labor, and capital declines.

The rapidity of this decline is regulated by the rate at which innovations are introduced. In industry the tendency toward diminishing returns is outweighed by the effects of technological progress and by the consequences of increasing returns to scale.

> The actual price of all commodities, excepting raw produce and labour, has a tendency to fall in the progress of wealth and population; for though, on one hand, they are enhanced in real value, from the rise in the natural price of the raw material of which they are made, this is more than counterbalanced by the improvements in machinery, by the better division and distribution of labour, and by the increasing skill, both in science and art of the producers.[4]

Historically, therefore, manufacturing will be subject to increasing returns.

In agriculture, however, Ricardo's assumption appears to have been that the rate innovations are introduced would not be sufficient to affect the tendency for diminishing returns to set in at either the intensive or the extensive margin of cultivation. Therefore, while the introduction of improvements in agricultural techniques might sporadically check the progress of diminishing returns, it could only exert a temporary effect upon costs of agricultural production. He wrote:

> With the progress of society the natural price of labour has always a tendency to rise, because one of the principal commodities by which its natural price is regulated (food) has a tendency to become dearer from the greater difficulty of producing it. As, however, the improvements in agriculture, the discovery of new markets whence provisions may be imported, may *for a time* counteract the tendency

> to a rise in the price of necessaries, and may even occasion their natural price to fall, so will the same causes produce the correspondent effects on the natural price of labour.[5]

Secularly, therefore, Ricardo assumed that in the production of food, diminishing returns would prevail. He postulated, in effect, that technological progress in agriculture was also subject to diminishing returns. Ricardo and his followers have often been taken to task for having underrated the possibility for technological advance in agriculture. Although historical evidence to date in advanced economies seems to dispute the validity of his hypothesis, it is quite conceivable that such a situation might arise at some future date. Furthermore, for underdeveloped economies, in which agricultural techniques have long remained stagnant, the Ricardian assumption seems to possess a significant degree of validity.

According to Ricardo, then, the historical pattern of real costs of production is the following: secularly, manufacturing is subject to increasing returns, whereas agriculture is subject to diminishing returns. With respect to the output of industry and agriculture together, which of these patterns prevails? Ricardo's reply to this question was that after all land has been taken into cultivation, the diminishing returns of agriculture more than outweigh the increasing returns of industry. As a result, from a certain historical date onward the rate of growth of output in expanding economies slows down; by the same token, the rate of diminution of output in declining economies decelerates.

Thus Ricardo wrote:

> Although, then, it is probable that, under the most favourable circumstances, the power of production is still greater than that of population, it will not long continue so; for the land being limited in quantity, and differing in quality, with every increased portion of capital employed on it there will be a decreased rate of production, whilst the power of population continues always the same.[6]

Unlike Adam Smith's economy, which grows at an accelerated rate, Ricardo's economy develops at a progressively slower historical pace.

The argument so far may be summarized in the following set of mathematical propositions. As before, we may write the production function as

$$Y = f(K, N, L) . \tag{4.1}$$

In addition, the class of admissible Ricardian production functions must be restricted to those for which marginal productivity is diminishing. That is, we require that

$$\frac{\partial^2 f}{\partial K^2} < 0\,, \tag{4.2}$$

$$\frac{\partial^2 f}{\partial N^2} < 0\,, \tag{4.3}$$

and

$$\frac{\partial^2 f}{\partial L^2} < 0\,. \tag{4.4}$$

Furthermore, since the pace of the economy's technological progress regulates to a large extent the rate of onset of diminishing returns, we may also write that

$$\frac{\partial^2 f}{\partial K^2} = g\left(\frac{dS}{dt}, \ldots\right), \tag{4.5}$$

$$\frac{\partial^2 f}{\partial N^2} = h\left(\frac{dS}{dt}, \ldots\right), \tag{4.6}$$

and

$$\frac{\partial^2 f}{\partial L^2} = j\left(\frac{dS}{dt}, \ldots\right). \tag{4.7}$$

Since dS/dt appears as one of the determinants of the extent of diminishing returns, it must also appear as a determinant of the marginal productivity of the factors of production themselves. We may simplify the mathematics somewhat by introducing S directly into the Ricardian production function. We shall therefore rewrite his production relationship (4.1) as

$$Y = f(K, N, L, S)\,. \tag{4.8}$$

One last word about the nature of the Ricardian production function is in order here. The assumption that with a given technology the coefficients of production are technically fixed has often been imputed to Ricardo. This interpretation, however, appears to do him less than justice. His arguments concerning the intensive margin of cultivation imply the possibility of adding different doses of labor and capital to a fixed amount of land. Therefore, at least the ratio of capital and labor to land is variable. Furthermore, there are also references to varying proportions between capital and labor in several passages. For example, Ricardo wrote:

> Now if the wages of labour rise 10 per cent and an additional capital of 500 1[ira]. be consequently required to enable him to employ the same labour, whilst his commodities continue to sell for 8000 1., he will no longer hesitate, but will at once purchase the machine, and will do the same annually, while wages continue above the original 5000 1.[7]

We see now that the Ricardian production function should not be restricted to one in which the technical coefficients are fixed.

To find the determinants of the economy's rate of progress we proceed as before. By differentiating production function (4.8) we get

$$\frac{dY}{dt} = \frac{\partial f}{\partial K}\frac{dK}{dt} + \frac{\partial f}{\partial N}\frac{dN}{dt} + \frac{\partial f}{\partial L}\frac{dL}{dt} + \frac{\partial f}{\partial S}\frac{dS}{dt}\,. \tag{4.9}$$

We must, therefore, investigate Ricardo's theory of capital accumulation (dK/dt), of land increase (dN/dt), of labor growth (dL/dt), and of technological progress (dS/dt).

NATURAL AND HUMAN RESOURCES

With respect to land, Ricardo was quite explicit. The factor land was defined by him to include only the "original and indestructible powers of the soil."[8] Therefore, he considered land to be fixed in supply,[9] or, expressed mathematically,

$$\frac{dN}{dt} = 0\,. \tag{4.10}$$

Ricardo's theory of population growth is similar, in general outline, to Adam Smith's. Like Smith, he distinguished between the market price of labor services and the "natural" wage rate. The latter concept is equivalent to Smith's subsistence wage: "The natural price of labour is that price which is necessary to enable the labourers, one with another, to subsist and to perpetuate their race, without either increase or diminution."[10] Market wages above the natural wage spur the growth of population; market wages below it discourage increases in numbers. Thus:

> It is when the market price of labour exceeds its natural price that the condition of the labourer is flourishing and happy, that he has it in his power to command a greater proportion of the necessaries and enjoyments of life, and therefore to rear a healthy and numerous family. When, however, by the encouragement which high wages give to the increase of population, the number of labourers is increased, wages again fall to their natural price, and indeed from a reaction sometimes fall below it. When the market price of labour is below its natural price, the condition of the labourers is most wretched: then poverty deprives them of those comforts which custom renders absolute necessaries. It is only after their privations have reduced their number, or the demand for labour has increased, that the market price of labour will rise to its natural price, and that the labourer will have the moderate comforts which the natural rate of wages will afford.[11]

We may therefore write that

$$\frac{dL_S}{dt} = Q[w - \bar{w}(t)] \leq \bar{Q}(t)\,, \tag{4.11}$$

where w and $\bar{w}(t)$ are, respectively, the market and the natural rates of wages at time t, and $\bar{Q}(t)$ is the maximum biologically possible rate of population growth at that time. Note that Ricardo's population function differs in several respects from Adam Smith's. First of all, in Ricardo the growth of labor is functionally related to (rather than, as in Smith, strictly proportional to) the difference between the market and the natural wage rates. Second, Ricardo postulated an explicit upper limit to the pace of population increase, a restriction that does not appear in Smith's treatment. Finally, whereas Smith's subsistence wage is physiologically determined and is therefore (in the absence of diminishing returns) constant through time, Ricardo's subsistence wage is historically variable.

If the demand for labor is growing at a faster rate than population can increase, money wages will exhibit a secular rise. Such a situation is typical of the beginning stages of development of virgin territories. "The productive powers of labour are generally greatest when there is an abundance of fertile land: at such periods accumulation is often so rapid that labourers cannot be supplied with the same rapidity as capital."[12] Therefore, "In new settlements, where the arts and knowledge of countries far advanced in refinement are introduced, it is probable that capital has a tendency to increase faster than mankind."[13]

As pointed out above, the natural wage rate changes through time. Two factors operate to raise it: First of all, the setting-in of diminishing returns in agriculture increases both the money and the real cost of the bundle of goods making up the subsistence level. "With the progress of society the natural price of labour has always a tendency to rise, because one of the principal commodities by which its natural price is regulated has a tendency to become dearer from the greater difficulty of producing it."[14] In addition, Ricardo recognized that the subsistence level itself is a socio-cultural phenomenon. He argued:

> It is not to be understood that the natural price of labour, estimated even in food and necessaries, is absolutely fixed and constant. It varies at different times in the same country, and very materially differs in different countries. It essentially depends on the habits and customs of the people. An English labourer would consider his wages under their natural rate, and too scanty to support a family, if they enabled him to purchase no other food than potatoes, and to live in no better habitation than a mud cabin; yet these moderate demands of nature are deemed sufficient in countries where "man's life is cheap" and his wants easily satisfied. Many of the conveniences now enjoyed in an English cottage would have been thought luxuries at an earlier period of our history.[15]

Ricardo's natural wage rate is therefore a function of the socio-cultural environment and of the marginal productivity of land. In fact, the variations of customs and agricultural productivity with time are responsible for the time-dependent behavior of the natural wage rate. Hence, it is more appropriate to express $\bar{w}$ not as an explicit function of t [as we did in (4.11)], but rather in the form

$$\bar{w} = \bar{w}\left(\frac{\partial f}{\partial N}, U\right). \tag{4.12}$$

Movements in the market rate of wages are regulated by the relationship of demand to supply. "The market price of labour is the price which is really paid for it, from the natural operation of the proportion of the supply to the demand."[16] Hence, if we denote the demand and supply of labor by L_D and L_S respectively, we may write that

$$w = w\left(\frac{L_D}{L_S}\right). \tag{4.13}$$

Wages rise when $L_D > L_S$; they are constant when $L_D = L_S$; and they fall when $L_D < L_S$.[17]

The demand for labor varies in proportion to changes in the capital stock of the community. "For in proportion to the increase in capital will be the increase in the demand for labour; in proportion to the work to be done will be the demand for those who are to do it."[18] That is,

$$\frac{dL_D}{dt} = q\,\frac{dK}{dt}, \tag{4.14}$$

where q is a constant greater than 0.

Generally, there is a tendency for the market rate of wages to conform to the natural rate. If demand exceeds supply, the market wage rises. High wages provide an impetus to population growth, which tends to reduce money wages. However, as long as the market wage is above subsistence the supply of labor continues to expand, forcing wages back toward a subsistence scale. Conversely, low wages tend to inhibit population expansion, thereby occasioning an analogous rise in wages toward their natural rate. Thus, "However much the market price of labour may deviate from its natural price, it has, like commodities, a tendency to conform to it."[19] In the long-run equilibrium, there is a balance between the expansion rate of the labor demand and the expansion rate of the labor supply. We have, then, that

$$\frac{dL_D}{dt} = \frac{dL_S}{dt} = \frac{dL}{dt} \tag{4.15}$$

on the average in the long run. Substituting (4.11) and (4.14) into (4.15), we get the labor market adjustment equation

$$Q\left[w - \bar{w}\left(\frac{\partial f}{\partial N}, U\right)\right] = q\,\frac{dK}{dt}. \tag{4.16}$$

This expression states that in the long run increases in the labor force are strictly proportional to increases in capital. "If the increase of capital be gradual and constant, the demand for labour may give a continued stimulus to an increase of people."[20] If, however, there is a rise in the natural wage rate (i.e., if $d\bar{w}/dt > 0$), the consequent increase in the supply of labor will fall short of the increase in demand, and the population will rise at a slower rate than capital. As a result, the market wage rate will rise and the rate of profit on capital will drop.[21] Equilibrium between the demand and supply of labor will again be restored by supply increasing faster and demand rising more slowly than before the rise in the subsistence wage.

Partially, of course [see equation (4.12)], an increase in the natural wage rate, measured either in money or in real cost, is merely a reflection of diminishing returns in agriculture. To the extent that this is the case, a rise in $\bar{w}$ does not reflect a net gain in living standards of the working classes. It serves merely to eat into entrepreneurial profits,* and thereby to slow down the future rate of capital accumulation and the rate of growth of the economy.

Such a rise in the natural wage rate is nobody's gain and somebody's loss. It is, therefore, undesirable from the point of view of society as a whole. For a time, this type of rise in the natural wage rate can be counteracted by improvements in agricultural technology[22] and by the importation of food.[23] However, Ricardo believed that these effects can succeed in counteracting the operation of diminishing returns only temporarily. Thus, in the long run: "Every exertion of industry, unless accompanied by a diminished rate of increase in population, will add to the evil, for production cannot keep pace with it."[24] It should be noted, though, that rises in $\bar{w}$ due to diminishing returns, while undesirable *per se,* create their own antidote insofar as they serve to lessen population pressures by lowering the rate of growth of population.

The welfare consequences for society are quite different when the rise in the natural wage rate results from the requirements of the working classes for higher universal standards of comforts and conveniences. The increase in natural wages then amounts to a real improvement in the living standards of the workers, who constitute "far the greatest part of every community."[25]

Let us now summarize Ricardo's theory of population. In general outline, it is quite similar to Adam Smith's theory. Both authors consider the rate of population growth to be geared to changes in demand,

---

* This will be discussed in more detail on pp. 54–55.

which, in turn, are geared to the rate of capital accumulation. And both authors relate the rate of population growth to the position of money wages relative to the subsistence wage. In contrast to Adam Smith, Ricardo considers the size of the subsistence wage to be a variable rather than a constant. This dependence, in Ricardo, of the natural wage rate upon the rate of diminishing returns from land and upon the socio-cultural setting permits policy manipulation of the rate of population growth in the economy. Population growth can be stimulated by the introduction of agricultural innovations and by the importation of foodstuffs from abroad. Or it can be slowed down by policy-induced subjective changes in minimal standards of living. An interesting sidelight upon the value judgments of this point is Ricardo's statement that "silks and velvets are not consumed by the labourer."[26]

CAPITAL ACCUMULATION

Let us turn now to an examination of Ricardo's theory of capital accumulation. Ricardo's definition of capital includes both the fixed and the circulating varieties. Thus he wrote: "Capital is that part of the wealth of a country which is employed in production, and consists of food, clothing, tools, raw materials, machinery, etc., necessary to give effect to labour."[27] The circulating capital constitutes the "wages fund"; it grows in constant proportion to fixed capital, except when capital-deepening technological change takes place.* Changes in the demand for labor, which are regulated by the increase of that portion of capital which constitutes the wages fund, are therefore (as explained earlier) generally in proportion to changes in the economy's capital stock.

"There are two ways," stated Ricardo, "in which capital may be accumulated; it may be saved either in consequence of increased revenue or of diminished consumption."[28] Whatever is saved is invested: "For no one accumulates but with a view to make his accumulation productive."[29] Thus no hoarding or dishoarding can intervene between *ex ante* savings and *ex post* investment.

---

* If capital-deepening occurs, the demand for labor rises at a slower rate than capital. We have ignored this possibility in the formal statement of Ricardo's theory, just as Ricardo did. However, its incorporation would not alter the qualitative nature of the argument. See Ricardo, *Principles,* pp. 270–71.

The rate of capital accumulation is regulated by two factors: the ability to save and the will to save. The first depends upon the amount of the surplus over the total product necessary to maintain labor's subsistence level, or the "net income" of the economy, as Ricardo called it.[30] The larger this surplus, the greater the means to save. For example: "Out of two loaves I may save one, out of four I may save three."[31] Naturally, a portion of the "net income" must go for the subsistence of the capitalist and landowner in any case.[32] But how large a fraction of their "net income" they consume is determined by the intensity of their motive for saving, that is to say, by the rate of profit. "While the profits of stock are high, men will have a motive to accumulate."[33] If the rate of profit falls, one can always turn toward increased consumption instead. "Whilst a man has any wished-for gratification unsupplied, he will have a demand for more commodities; and it will be an effectual demand while he has any new value to offer in exchange for them."[34]

But how does the rate of savings vary with the rate of profit? Is it a negative function of the rate of profits as Adam Smith wrote? No, said Ricardo. Men's motives for capital accumulation "will diminish with every diminution of profit, and will cease altogether when profits are so low as not to afford them an adequate compensation for their trouble, and the risk which they must necessarily encounter in employing their capital productively."[35]

Symbolically, Ricardo's theory of capital accumulation may be summarized as follows:

$$\frac{dK}{dt} = k(r - \bar{r}, Y - \bar{w}L)\,, \tag{4.17}$$

where $(Y - \bar{w}L)$ is the community's "net income," and r and $\bar{r}$ are, respectively, the actual and the minimal rate of profits. Ricardo also placed restrictions upon the shape of (4.17), in that $\partial k/\partial(r - \bar{r}) > 0$ and $\partial k/\partial(Y - \bar{w}L) > 0$. Given the rate of profits, then, it is apparent from (4.17) that capital grows with the economy's net income.* And, given "net income," capital accumulation is an increasing function of the difference between actual profits and the minimal compensation

* In equation (4.17) it is not assumed that, given the rate of interest, the marginal propensity to save equals the average propensity to save.

for risk. Furthermore, according to Ricardo, two things can choke off capital accumulation entirely: a net surplus of zero above subsistence, and a fall in the rate of profits to the minimally acceptable rate. The conditions under which these two eventualities arise are not, however, independent. As will be apparent later, they are both related to the productivity of land at the margin of cultivation.

To determine the dynamic course of capital accumulation in a Ricardian economy, we must examine the behavior through time of the system's "net income" and its rate of profits. Ricardo's theory of profits has been subject to much discussion. His use of the terms "profits" and "wages" (unless clearly labeled as the rate of profits and the rate or price of wages) referred to the relative share of profits and to the relative share of wages at the margin.[36] Since at the margin no rent is paid,[37] profits (in the Ricardian sense) depend only upon wages (and vice versa, of course). Therefore, the Ricardian dictum that "nothing can affect profits but a rise in wages"[38] is merely a truism. With this definition, profits can be determined as a residual over and above wages on that portion of land which yields no rent.

However, it is not the actual wage payment that determines profits in the Ricardian sense; rather, it is the subsistence wage. The explanation of this statement is, once again, a matter of definition. In discussions concerning the impact of profits upon capital accumulation, Ricardo preferred to consider the portion of wages that is over and above subsistence as part of profits rather than as part of wages. Thus, he wrote to Malthus: "The wages themselves may be considered as part of the profits of stock—and are frequently the foundation of new capital."[39] In this way he could consider workers' savings, as well as the savings of other classes of society, to be determined by profits. Given these definitions, Ricardo's statement that "in all countries, and all times, profits depend on the quantity of labour requisite to provide necessaries for the labourers on that land or with that capital which yields no rent"[40] follows as an identity. No wonder then that Ricardo was bitter about having been attacked on this score!

Provided that capital and labor move in constant proportion to each other[41] (which Ricardo assumed for the long run), the rate of profit would rise and fall according to whether the subsistence wage rate fell or rose. In mathematical notation

$$r = m(\bar{w})\,. \tag{4.18}$$

As a result, he argued that the "natural tendency of profits is to fall; for, in the progress of society and wealth, the additional quantity of food required is obtained by the sacrifice of more and more labour." Periodically, the tendency toward diminishing returns is checked by the introduction of technological innovations. This lowers the share of subsistence wages in total output at the margin of cultivation. During these periods, profits rise. However, since Ricardo believed that technological progress is also subject to diminishing returns, the long-run trend of profits will be downward.[42] At first, the rate at which profits fall due to diminishing returns is sufficiently slow to permit the share of profits in total output to increase. At the beginning stages of growth, therefore, capital accumulation proceeds at an accelerated pace.[43] The downward pressure upon capital accumulation exerted by the falling rate of profits is outweighed by the upward pull of a larger net surplus above subsistence.

However, as society expands, the share of profits in total output begins to drop.[44] The rate of capital accumulation slows down. Ultimately, as the pressure of an increasingly larger population requires the cultivation of poorer and poorer land, the portion of the product at the margin swallowed up by the subsistence wage becomes so great that profits approach $\bar{r}$. When this happens, capital accumulation stops, population remains constant, and the economy enters the stationary state. The dynamic time path of capital, as visualized by Ricardo, is portrayed in Fig. 4.1.

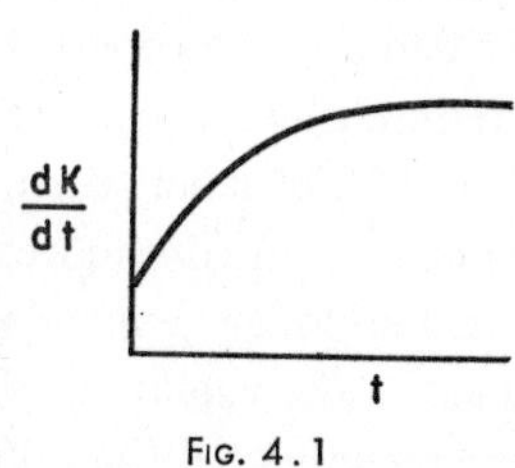

Fig. 4.1

THE PATTERN OF DEVELOPMENT

We may now summarize the dynamic process as Ricardo visualized it. The normal progress of this economy toward the stationary state is punctuated by periods of temporary equilibrium, during which wages are at the subsistence level and population is stationary. However, since during these periods the economy's "*net* income" is positive and the rate of returns on investment is above $\bar{r}$, these temporary equilibria cannot persist. New investment is taking place, which raises the demand for labor, driving wages above subsistence. As a result, population increases. Meanwhile, the temporary rise in wages lowers the rate of profit. This leads to a slower rate of capital accumulation.

When the supply of labor has finally caught up to its demand, a new equilibrium position is attained. Wages fall to subsistence. This raises the rate of profit above $\bar{r}$. As a result, a renewed stimulus is imparted to capital accumulation, and a process similar to that described above starts all over again. The progress of the economy since the previous equilibrium state may be described by the simultaneous solution of (4.9), (4.10), and (4.16), which gives

$$\frac{dY}{dt} = \left(\frac{\partial f}{\partial K} + q\,\frac{\partial f}{\partial L}\right)\frac{dK}{dt} + \frac{\partial f}{\partial S}\,\frac{dS}{dt}\,. \tag{4.19}$$

It is apparent from (4.19) that the rate of capital accumulation plays a significant role in determining the pace of economic progress. But now the development of the economy is affected by changes in $\bar{w}$, through their impact upon dK/dt [equation (4.17)]. When subsistence wages increase, the rate of profit drops, and therefore the rate of capital accumulation is reduced from the value it would have had under a constant $\bar{w}$. Hence, the rate of growth of labor will be reduced by an increase in subsistence costs. With a positive marginal product of labor, then, the rate of increase of the total product will be lower. Furthermore, unlike the Smithian economy, the Ricardian system no longer expands or decays strictly according to its rate of investment. The evolution of the economy is modified by the growth rate of the accumulated fund of knowledge of society, dS/dt. Even when the capital stock does not increase, technological improvements increase the marginal productivity of capital and labor [see equations (4.5)–(4.7)] at the intensive and extensive margins of cultivation of land. This results in a larger output, even with the same doses of the production factors. In addition, technological improvements serve to retard the progress of diminishing returns, as stated earlier.

The economy's successive equilibrium positions differ from each other with respect to the sizes of their populations and capital stocks. Since agricultural production is subject to historically diminishing returns, the larger population can be supported on the same amount of land only at an increasing real cost. Output, at the margin of cultivation, diminishes. Moreover, an increasing share of the marginal output must be paid out in wages to labor for its subsistence. This drives the rate of profits down and slows up capital accumulation.[45] Unlike the Smithian economy, then, which races toward the stationary state, the Ricardian system approaches it at a successively slower pace.

Furthermore, the progress of the economy toward the stationary state "is happily checked at repeated intervals by improvements in machinery connected with the production of necessaries, as well as by discoveries in the science of agriculture."[46] These counteract, for a time, the action of diminishing returns. Under the impact of technological progress, the secular rate of profit may even rise for considerable periods. At such times the rate of capital accumulation may outstrip the biologically possible rate of population growth,[47] driving (and keeping) real wages above subsistence for extended periods of time. In the end, however, as the impetus from technological progress is exhausted, diminishing returns again take over, and the economy resumes its sedate motion toward the stationary state.

What are the properties of the Ricardian stationary state? "The very low rate of profits will have arrested all accumulation";[48] thus, "no additional labour can be demanded, and consequently population will have reached its highest point."[49] Constant capital, maximum population, wages at subsistence, profits at a minimum consistent with compensation for risk, and a stationary total product—these characterize the traits of the Ricardian stationary state.

Not all stationary states are equivalent, however. It will be recalled that in Ricardo the level of subsistence required by the workers is, in part, a socio-cultural phenomenon. Let us therefore consider two communities, identical in all respects except that community A demands a higher subsistence level than community B. Capital accumulation and growth will therefore be choked off sooner in A than in B. The "maximum" population of A will be smaller than that of B, but the workers of A will have a higher standard of living than the workers of B. Therefore, Ricardo considered stationary state A superior to stationary state B. He accepted the value judgment (implicit in current economic development literature) that greater happiness for a smaller society is superior to less happiness for a larger number of people. As a result:

> The friends of humanity cannot but wish that in all countries the labouring classes should have a taste for comforts and enjoyments, and that they should be stimulated by all legal means in their exertions to procure them. There cannot be a better security against a

> superabundant population. In those countries where the labouring classes have fewer wants and are contented with the cheapest food, the people are exposed to the greatest vicissitudes and miseries.[50]

The stationary state was "as yet far distant,"[51] according to Ricardo. The analogous condition of underdevelopment could, however, be observed in practical economies of his time. Accordingly, Ricardo distinguished between two types of underdeveloped economies: On the one hand, "those countries where there is abundance of fertile land, but where, from the ignorance, indolence, barbarism of the inhabitants, they are exposed to all the evils of want and famine, and where it has been said that population presses against the means of subsistence";[52] and on the other hand, "long settled countries, where, from the diminishing rate of the supply of raw produce, all the evils of a crowded population are experienced." The first of Ricardo's prototypes corresponds to an underpopulated economy; the second is the case of an overpopulated underdeveloped community.

These cases must be distinguished from each other for policy purposes. The sparsely populated case requires a more rapid rate of capital accumulation. This can be brought about by exogenous shifts in S and in U. Changes in the society's accumulated fund of knowledge will raise r by lowering the cost of subsistence $\bar{w}$. And variations in the institutional setting will also serve to lower the risk premium necessary for investment, and thereby reduce $\bar{r}$. Therefore, Ricardo argued:

> In the one case, the evil proceeds from bad government, from the insecurity of property, and from a want of education in all ranks of the people. To be made happier, they require only to be better governed and instructed, as the augmentation of capital, beyond the augmentation of people, would be the inevitable result.

The other case, that of a densely populated underdeveloped economy, is a more hopeless one. In such an economy, an increase in capital will only make matters worse, for the increase in capital will call forth a growth in population. Thus, it will merely add to the pressure upon scarce land resources. Therefore, in densely populated countries, "Every exertion of industry, unless accompanied by a diminished rate of increase in the population, will add to the evil, for production cannot keep pace with it." The only remedy in this case is population control This can be achieved by raising the economic aspirations of the lower classes of society. In other words, a culturally induced increase in $\bar{w}$ is Ricardo's policy recommendation for this case.

In summary, the Ricardian dynamic path for Y may be derived from the simultaneous solution of the rate of growth of output equation (4.19) and the rate of capital accumulation equation (4.17), subject to the other stated restrictions upon the system. We may express this solution symbolically as

$$(4.20) \qquad Y = y[K_0, N_0, L_0 ; \alpha_1, \ldots, \alpha_N ; \overline{U}(t) ; \overline{S}(t)] .$$

As before, the solution depends upon the initial conditions (K_0, N_0, L_0) and upon the structural parameters of the economy ($\alpha_1, \ldots, \alpha_N$). In addition, we also have two policy variables, $\overline{U}(t)$ and $\overline{S}(t)$, both of which are exogenously determined.

The influence of the socio-cultural environment is felt through its impact upon $\bar{w}$ [equation (4.12)]. By affecting the economy's subjective minimal standards of living, changes in outlook and in institutions can modify the rates of growth of the labor force, of investment, and therefore of output, and the nature of the stationary state of the economy. Even more important, perhaps, is the role of changes in the fund of applied knowledge of society in conditioning economic development. As we saw from equations (4.5)–(4.7), dS/dt participates in the determination of the productivities of the factors of production. In addition, it is apparent from (4.6) and (4.12) that technological factors influence the time path of the subsistence wage. Finally, S also modifies the rate of capital accumulation through its impact upon r [see equation (4.18)] and upon the Ricardian net income ($Y - \bar{w}L$) of the community. The influence of technological factors therefore permeates the entire Ricardian economy.

Underdevelopment may be remedied by exogenous shifts in one or both of these policy variables. In the case of a sparsely populated economy, primary reliance should be placed on shifts in S. The Ricardian answer to the problem of a densely populated underdeveloped system, on the other hand, lies in exogenous shifts in U. By raising $\bar{w}$, changes in outlook will reduce both population and capital. However, per capita output will increase, since the marginal land under cultivation will now be more productive.

FIVE

KARL MARX

IN THIS CHAPTER we shall examine Karl Marx's theory of growth. We shall see that it is based upon a particular set of assumptions concerning the nature of production functions, the character of innovations, and the manner of capital accumulation. Taken together, these assumptions imply something concerning the behavior of wage rates and of profit rates through time; they therefore have certain consequences for the dynamic behavior of the economy. In particular, they imply the existence of structural maladjustments in a growing economy. They suggest, furthermore, that the system is explosive in nature.

In analyzing the economic theories of the classical writers, we focused primarily upon the question, "What did these authors tell us about the nature of economic growth and development?" Accordingly, we were not vitally concerned with the universality of the models they presented. It was understood that Smith and Ricardo described economic progress in specific types of economies, and that their generalizations were valid only to the extent that their particular postulates were applicable. In our analysis of the Marxian model, however, we shall be somewhat more ambitious—first, we shall ask whether, given the nature of Marx's postulates, his system is internally consistent. Then, in view of the importance of Marxian theory in the world today, we shall inquire whether the empirical evidence provided by the economic development of industrial economies supports the generalizations contained in Marx's postulates.

Much of the discussion of Marx has concerned the validity of his labor theory of value. We shall not investigate this problem at all, since we concur with Fellner, who wrote:

> The main function of the labour-value theory in Marx's work is that of linking a set of hypotheses to a "creed" in which the judgment is prominent that all non-labour income results from "exploitation,"

and hence is objectionable. This note [of Fellner's] is concerned with Marxian hypotheses rather than with the creed to which they are linked. In the interpretation of the hypotheses themselves it is desirable to bypass the labour-value theory, which, after all, is a very confusing theory.[1]

PRODUCTIVE ACTIVITIES OF AN ECONOMY

Marx devoted considerable attention to the analysis of the productive activities of an economy. "The elementary factor of the labour-process," he wrote, "are 1, the personal activity of man, *i.e.*, work itself, 2, the subject of that work, and 3, its instruments,"[2] As Marx visualized it: "Labour is, in the first place, a process in which . . . man of his own accord starts, regulates, and controls the material re-actions between himself and Nature."[3] In addition, however, labor has a social character: "The relation of the producers to the sum total of their labour is presented to them as a social relation, existing not between themselves, but between the products of their labour."[4]

The primary resource upon which human labor is expended is land. For Marx, land includes the "subjects of labour spontaneously provided by Nature," as well as the raw materials that have "been filtered through previous labour"; the instruments of labor are "a thing, or a complex of things, which the labourer interposes between himself and the subject of his labour, and which serves as the conductor of his activity."[5] The productivity of labor, however, depends also upon "the degree of development, greater or less, in the form of social production"; hence, labor productivity "is a gift, not of nature, but of a history embracing thousands of centuries."[6]

We see, then, that the social and historical character of production is an integral part of Marx's point of view.[7] Symbolically, his theory of the production process may be summarized in our notation by

$$Y = f(K, N, L, S, U)\,, \tag{5.1}$$

as in the general case of Chapter Two. In this expression, however, it is necessary (in order to correspond to Marx's theory) to expand the meaning of S beyond that which has so far been assigned to it. In addition to being an index of the accumulated fund of applied technical knowledge, the index S must include some measure of the interaction between techniques of production and the social and economic organization of society. For example, the old plantation system in the southern part of the United States used techniques of production involving slave labor. The social implications of slavery from the Marxian point of view must therefore be incorporated in some manner into the determination of the value of S corresponding to these techniques.

The index S thus reflects both the method of production in use at a given time and the economic and social relationships that these methods imply. It corresponds to the Marxian concept of "relations of production," which, according to Bober,

> refer to an organic whole uniquely characterized by the following components: (1) the organization of labor in a scheme of division and cooperation, the skills of labor, and the status of labor in the social context with respect to degrees of freedom or servitude; (2) the geographical environment and the knowledge of the use of resources and materials; and (3) technical means and processes and the state of science generally.[8]

According to Marx, the relations of production* determine the entire social, cultural, legal, and institutional structure of society. For, as he explained in his famous Preface to *The Critique of Political Economy:*

> In the social production of their means of existence men enter into definite, necessary relations which are independent of their will, productive relationships which correspond to a definite stage of development of their material productive forces. The aggregate of these productive relationships constitutes the economic structure of society, the real basis on which a juridical and political superstructure arises, and to which definite forms of social consciousness correspond. The mode of production of the material means of existence conditions the whole process of social, political and intellectual life. It is not the consciousness of men that determines their existence, but, on the contrary, it is their social existence that determines their consciousness.[9]

Or, in the words of Engels:

---

* Since Marx himself seems never to have defined the concept of "relations of production," his followers' pronouncements on the matter are subject to various interpretations. However, Bober's interpretation of this phrase seems reasonable, and will be used in the remainder of this chapter. For a detailed discussion of this concept and its interpretations, see R. N. Carew Hunt, *Marxism Past and Present* (New York: Macmillan and Co., 1955), pp. 49 ff.

> The materialist conception of history starts from the principle that production, and with production the exchange of its products, is the basis of every social order; that in every society which has appeared in history the distribution of the products, and with it the division of society into classes or estates, is determined by what is produced and how it is produced, and how the product is exchanged. According to this conception, the ultimate cause of all social changes and political revolutions are to be sought, not in the minds of men, in their increasing insight into eternal truth and justice, but in changes in the mode of production and exchange; they are to be sought not in the *philosophy* but in the *economics* of the epoch concerned.[10]

THEORY OF SOCIAL EVOLUTION

Since the relations of production are continually changing, Marx's theory of social evolution is, by its very essence, dynamic in nature. Marx stated: "There is a continual movement of growth in productive forces, of destruction in the social relations, of formation in ideas; the only immutable thing is the abstraction of movement—*mors immortalis*."[11] Such a concept of continuous change is inherent in the dialectic approach, which is "nothing more than the science of the general laws of motion and development of Nature, human society and thought."[12] This Hegelian thesis consists of

> the great basic thought that the world is not to be comprehended as a complex of ready made *things,* but as a complex of *processes,* in which the things apparently stable no less than their mind-images in our heads, the concepts, go through an uninterrupted change of coming into being and passing away, in which, in spite of all seeming accidents and of all temporary retrogression, a progressive development asserts itself in the end.[13]

The dynamic process arises as a result of the existence of internal contradictions. As explained by Engels:

> Motion itself is a contradiction: even simple mechanical change of place can only come about through a body at one and the same moment of time being both in one place and in another place, being in one and the same place and also not in it. And the continuous assertion and simultaneous solution of this contradiction is precisely what motion is.[14]

Evolution and growth are thus by their very essence disequilibrium phenomena.

In the social sphere, the disequilibrium (and hence the progress) arises from the fact that there exists a lag in the adaptation of the legal, institutional, social, and cultural framework of society to its mode of production. Today's ideas and political setup are appropriate to the requirements of yesterday's productive forces. Therefore, after a certain evolution in the relations of production has taken place,* a conflict will develop between the socio-cultural environment and the further growth of the productive powers of the economy. At this point, the existing organizational and ideological structure of society begins to crumble; it is soon replaced by new institutions more favorable to the growth of the productive possibilities of the economy. In Marx's own words:

> At a certain stage of their development the material productive forces of society come into contradiction with the existing productive relationships, or, what is but a legal expression for these, with the property relationships within which they had moved before. From forms of development of the productive forces these relationships are transformed into their fetters. Then an epoch of social revolution opens. With the change in the economic foundation the whole vast superstructure is more or less rapidly transformed.[15]

But Marx warned that "No social order ever disappears before all the productive forces, for which there is room in it, have been developed, and new higher relations of production never appear before the material conditions of their existence have matured in the womb of the old society."[16] Therefore, as Engels put it:

> The growing realization that existing social institutions are irrational and unjust, that reason has become nonsense and good deeds a scourge, is only a sign that changes have been taking place quietly in the methods of production and forms of exchange with which the social order, adapted to previous economic conditions, is no longer in accord.[17]

Mathematically, this theory may be expressed as

$$U = g\left(S, \frac{dS}{dt}, \frac{d^2S}{dt^2}, \ldots, t\right), \tag{5.2}$$

* For Marx, technical progress does not always proceed at a uniform pace through time. Rather, it is subject to discrete shifts, superimposed upon smooth growth.

since lags in the impact of S upon U can be placed in the general form (5.2). If we insert this relationship into production function (5.1), we may simply drop U and write

$$Y = h\left(K, N, L, S, \frac{dS}{dt}, \frac{d^2S}{dt^2}, \ldots, t\right). \tag{5.3}$$

Historical Evolution Theory. Marx and Engels applied this philosophy of dialectic materialism to the anaylsis of the historical evolution of humanity. In broad outlines, they distinguished four different stages through which the relations of production (and hence society) have passed: primitive communism (or the Asiatic stage), slavery (the ancient stage), feudalism, and capitalism.

The state of primitive communism is characterized by a classless society in which all output is owned in common and the only division of labor occurs between the sexes: "The man wages war, goes hunting and fishing, procures the raw material of food and the tools required for these. The woman looks after the house and the preparation of food and clothing, cooks, weaves and sews."[18] With the discovery of the possibility of domesticating and breeding wild animals, the first step in the specialization of labor was taken when pastoral tribes separated themselves from other tribes. This development enabled exchange to take place. Also, horticulture, the forerunner of agriculture, made its appearance toward the end of this stage. At the same time, the weaving loom and the smelting of ores were discovered.

These new production possibilities "gave human labour power the capacity to produce a larger product than was necessary for its maintenance."[19] They also increased the demand for labor, to an extent which could not be fully satisfied under the existing form of society. "In the general historical conditions then prevailing the first great social division of labour, with its increase of the productivity of labour and therefore of wealth, and its widening field of production, necessarily brought slavery in its train."[20] Primitive communism gave way to the second stage—slavery.

In this period, slavery was the dominant relation of production. Labor became more specialized; further division of work, especially between town and country, took place. Exchange flourished, and a class of merchants who acted as intermediaries between producers arose. The institutions of metallic money, private ownership of land, interest, mortgages, and testamentary procedures were introduced. States emerged out of the need to provide a system of checks and balances among the divergent interests of the classes of this more complex society.[21]

As the productive forces developed further, feudalism replaced slavery. In the countryside, the prevalent form of production was serfdom, in which the serf was tied to the land but had a certain amount of personal dignity. Agriculture and handicraft industries—characterized by small-scale production based on the private ownership by the workers of their instruments and means of production—emerged in town and country. The guild system came into being. However, as production and exchange expanded, the feudal political form became a hindrance to the further growth of the productive powers of the economy.

> In all their production the burghers had remained hemmed in by the feudal political forms of the Middle Ages, which this production —not only manufacture, but even handicraft industry—had long outgrown: they were still entangled in all the thousandfold guild privileges and local provincial customs barriers which had become mere irritants and fetters on production.[22]

Furthermore, in view of the private ownership of the instruments and objects of labor, the scale of production was "necessarily puny, dwarfish, restricted." Feudalism could not meet this challenge; therefore:

> To concentrate and enlarge these scattered, limited means of production, to transform them into the mighty levers of production of the present day, was precisely the historic role of the capitalist mode of production and of its representative, the bourgeoisie. . . . The mode of production peculiar to the bourgeoisie—called, since Marx, the capitalist mode of production—was incompatible with the local privileges and the privileges of birth as well as with the reciprocal personal ties of the feudal system; [therefore] the bourgeoisie shattered the feudal system, and on its ruins established the bourgeois social order, the realm of free competition, freedom of movement, equal rights for commodity owners and all the other bourgeois glories. The capitalist mode of production could now develop freely.[23]

Characteristic of this mode of production is the fact that the worker himself no longer owns the agents of production. A class of capitalists, who are owners of the means and the instruments of production and a propertyless, but free proletariat emerge. According to Marx:

> The capitalist system presupposes the complete separation of the labourers from all property in the means by which they can realise their labours. . . . The process, therefore, that clears the way for the capitalist system, can be none other than the process which takes away from the labourer the possession of his means of production; a process that transforms, on the one hand, the social means of subsistence and of production into capital, on the other, the immediate producers into wage-labourers.[24]

The technical conditions of production undergo a vast transformation from handicraft cottage industries to manufacture and, later, to "machine-facture." With capital and paid labor, industry now assumes the character of production for the market place. Under manufacturing, "the spindles and looms, formerly scattered over the face of the country, are now crowded together in a few great labour-barracks, together with the labourers and the raw material."[25] We now have more intensive division of labor and complete divorce of manufacturing from agriculture.

Later, the industrial revolution introduces the machine, and correspondingly improves large-scale production techniques. The result: more centralization, more elaborate marketing and financial institutions, a predominance of industrial over financial capital, monopoly, increasing inequalities of income, and colonialism.

> Hand in hand with this centralisation, or this expropriation of many capitalists by few, develop on an ever expanding scale the co-operative form of the labour-process, the conscious technical application of science, the methodical cultivation of the soil, the transformation of the instruments of labour into instruments of labour only usable in common, the economising of all means of production by their use as the means of production of combined, socialised labour, the entanglement of all peoples into the net of the world market, and this, the international character of the capitalistic regime.[26]

Gradually, this system, too, develops internal contradictions.

> The monopoly of capital becomes a fetter upon the mode of production, which has sprung up and flourished along with, and under it. Centralisation of the means of production and socialisation of labour at last reach a point where they become incompatible with their capitalistic integument. This integument bursts asunder. The knell

of capitalistic private property sounds. The expropriators are expropriated.[27]

Summary of Theory of Historical Process. This, then, is the Marxian version of the historical process: economic factors play the decisive role in shaping the evolution of society, because the relations of production determine the ideological, political, legal, and institutional structure of the community. Since technology is continually changing, the form society takes is also subject to constant modification. Indeed, one may identify four different historical stages, each of which arose out of the previous stage as a result of the conflict between the forces of production and the legal, institutional, and cultural framework in which they evolved. In each case the internal contradictions generated by this incompatibility led to the breakdown of the older system and to the emergence of a new one. In each instance, the agents of change were the social classes that were created by the particular mode of production that was used; the method of change was a struggle between classes arising from the internal contradictions of the system. Nor is the capitalist mode of production exempt from this disease. It, too, has created its internal stresses and strains. Like the previous stages, therefore it will eventually be swept away, according to Marx, in favor of other forms—socialism at first, and then communism.

Critique of Marxian Interpretation of History. How valid is Marx's interpretation of history? Like all single-factor explanations, his economic interpretation fails to account for all the complexities of the social and historical process. Further, it suffers from the deficiencies of other "stage" theories of history: social evolution is almost always more gradual than such theories would allow, and elements characteristic of one stage often appear in a prior stage or persist into the subsequent one. On the other hand, as concluded by Professor See:

> The economic interpretation of history is on solid ground. There is no doubt that economic phenomena exert considerable influence on the progress of history. How can we really understand the organisation of any society if we do not know the organisation of labour, the system of industry, the commercial customs, the agrarian regime, etc.? This is true of all epochs. . . . If it is too much to claim that religious phenomena have been determined by economic causes, it is certain that they have in many cases been influenced by the

geographical environment and the social organisation. . . . In spite of the criticism that may be directed against the materialistic conception of history, it must be admitted that it contains a large element of truth. Furthermore, it has effectively stimulated investigations in economic history. For the last half century in fact, many historians have pronounced in favor of the economic interpretation of history without in any way accepting the social doctrine of Marxism.[28]

COURSE OF PRODUCTION

To return to the main thread of the argument, we have seen that, in Marx, the historical development of a society is uniquely determined by the manner in which the economy carries on its productive activities. To understand the social history of a community, then, one must study the evolution through time of its production processes. Therefore, we must undertake a more detailed investigation of the course of production in a Marxian system.

According to Marx, the gross output of an economy is composed of three elements. The first is the variable capital (v, in Marx's notation), or the wage bill, which corresponds to the classical circulating capital or wages fund. Next we have the constant capital (c, in Marx), which is composed of the plant and raw materials used up in production; i.e., the depreciation of physical plant and equipment and the consumption of the intermediate goods employed in the production process. The term "constant capital" is applied to this portion of the economy's capital stock because "it adds no more to the value of output than it loses in production, new value added being due to the labour-power purchased by variable capital."[29]

Finally, there is the surplus value (s, in Marx's terminology), or the value added in production. For Marx, the "absolute amount of profit is equal to the absolute amount of surplus value,"[30] which arises because, as will be explained later, the worker does not receive the entire value of his marginal product in wages. Indeed, he is paid only his subsistence wage. Since Marx postulated that at any given point of time t production takes place with constant coefficients, we may rewrite his production function as

$$Y = (q_1 + q_2)L + kK + nN \,, \tag{5.4}$$

where q_1L represents Marx's variable capital v, q_2L is the surplus value, and $(kK + nN)$ corresponds to Marx's constant capital c. Note that Marx always treats $(kK + nN)$ as the single quantity c; consequently, it will be convenient to combine the equipment and raw material components of the production function into one index K', and to replace the production function (5.4) by

$$Y = (q_1 + q_2)L + k'K'. \tag{5.5}$$

The coefficients of production (q_1, q_2, k') are not fixed over time—they vary as the relations of production change. Indeed, Marx treats changes in the ratios of these coefficients as functions *solely* of the relations of production.[31] Although he does not explicitly discuss the coefficients of production themselves, there is no evidence to indicate that he considered them individually to depend strongly upon the other variables of the system. Therefore we may write

$$q_1 = q_1(S), \tag{5.6}$$

$$q_2 = q_2(S), \tag{5.7}$$

and

$$k' = k'(S). \tag{5.8}$$

As a result, the rate of expansion of the economy's output becomes

$$\frac{dY}{dt} = [q_1(S) + q_2(S)]\frac{dL}{dt} + k'(S)\frac{dK'}{dt} + \left[L\frac{d(q_1 + q_2)}{dS} + K'\frac{dk'}{dS}\right]\frac{dS}{dt}. \tag{5.9}$$

To determine the time path of the economy's rate of production, then, we must examine the development of the relations of production as well as the progress through time of the amount of labor employed and of the equipment and raw materials used up.

Technical Change. Let us first look at the relations of production. Improvements in production techniques are regulated by the gross rate of capital formation in the economy, since any piece of capital equipment actually in operation requires fixed amounts of labor to work it.[32] Therefore, it is only when new pieces of capital equipment are introduced or when old machinery is replaced that changes in the proportions of capital to labor employed are at all possible. The rate of innovation is consequently governed by the gross rate of addition to the capital stock of the economy. "The additional capitals formed in the course of accumulation . . . serve mainly as vehicles for the exploitation of new inventions and discoveries, or of industrial improvements in general."[33] We therefore have the proposition that

$$\frac{dS}{dt} = Z(I)\,, \tag{5.10}$$

where I stands for gross investment. Marx also implies that the rate of change of the relations of production is an increasing function of the amount of gross investment; that is, $dZ/dI > 0$.

Modifications in the economy's technology are reflected in variations through time of the coefficients of production [see equations (5.6)–(5.8)]. Marx postulated that, generally speaking, technological progress is labor-displacing. That is, he assumed that the techniques of production become more capital-intensive with the passage of time. As an index of this effect Marx used the ratio of constant to variable capital c/v, which he called the "organic composition of Capital."[34] This ratio measures the capital and raw materials used per worker employed[35] or "the mass of means of production, as compared with the mass of the labour-power that vivifies them."[36]

Marx believed that the organic composition of capital rises through time. He deduced "this law of progressive increase in constant capital, in proportion to the variable" from the postulate of a long-run trend toward an increasing productivity of labor. He argued, first of all, that, since an increase in labor productivity signifies that the same amount of labor produces a larger quantity of output, it also implies that "a greater mass of raw material and auxiliary substances enter into the labour-process." Second, the increase in productivity occurs only as a result of a larger proportion of capital equipment per worker. Therefore:

> Whether condition or consequence, the growing extent of the means of production, as compared with the labour-power incorporated with them, is an expression of the growing productiveness of labour. The increase of the latter appears, therefore, in the diminution of the mass of labour in proportion to the mass of means of production

moved by it, or in the diminution of the subjective factor of the labour process as compared with the objective factor.

It is interesting to note that Marx deduced this tendency toward a secular rise in the organic composition of capital without directly analyzing the course of either interest rates or wage rates. The rate of change of c/v (which determines the rate or pace at which the relative displacement of labor in production occurs) depends solely upon the rate of change of technology, which, in turn, depends upon the rate of gross capital formation. If we denote the organic composition of capital at time t by b, we may write that

$$(5.11) \qquad \frac{db}{dt} = m\left(\frac{ds}{dt}\right) = m'(I)\,,$$

where m and m' are secularly positive. As we shall see below, $\partial I/\partial t > 0$. Therefore,

$$(5.12) \qquad \frac{db}{dI} = \frac{db/dt}{dI/dt} > 0\,.$$

That is to say, the organic composition of capital is an increasing function of the rate of gross capital formation. The greater the rate of gross investment, the more rapid the increase of the constant capital stock compared with the variable.

The Demand for Labor. The rate of increase of the variable capital stock also regulates the demand for labor, for it will be recalled that the total product of labor $[(q_1 + q_2)L]$ may be divided into two parts. These parts are (1) $q_1L = v$, the variable capital, which represents the wage bill, or the portion of the labor output paid to the workers, and (2) $q_2L = s$, the surplus value, or the portion of the labor product accruing to the capitalists. Marx equated the ratio $s/v = q_2/q_1$ to the rate of exploitation of labor power by capital.[37] Whenever the rate of exploitation of labor and the productivity of labor are both constant, q_1 is fixed and the increase in demand for labor moves in exact proportion to the increase in variable capital. For, by the definition of v,

$$(5.13) \qquad L = \frac{v}{q_1(S)}\,.$$

Therefore, on the demand side,*

* In Marx the supply of labor is exogenously determined. See below, p. 74.

$$(5.14) \qquad \frac{dL}{dt} = \frac{q_1(dv/dt) - v(dq_1/dt)}{(q_1)^2}.$$

If $dq_1/dt = 0$, that is, if q_1 is constant, then the demand for labor increases proportionately with changes in variable capital. On the other hand, if q_1 goes up through time, the demand for labor rises more slowly than the variable component of capital. Such a secular increase in q_1 will occur if either (a) the productivity of labor increases, the rate of exploitation remaining the same, or (b) the rate of exploitation rises, with productivity staying unchanged. Since Marx believed that both the productivity of labor and the rate of labor exploitation tend to rise secularly,[38] he expected that a secular increase in q_1 would take place, and hence that the demand for labor would usually rise more slowly than the variable capital.[39] His views of the technical relationships involved in production imply further that the labor–capital ratio depends only on the history of gross investment, since, from the definition of variable capital (5.13) and the definition of constant capital

$$(5.15) \qquad K' = \frac{c}{k'(S)},$$

one may write

$$(5.16) \qquad \frac{L}{K'} = \frac{q_1(S)k'(S)}{c/v}.$$

If we integrate (5.11), we find*

$$(5.17) \qquad \frac{c}{v} = b = b\left(I, \frac{dI}{dt}, \frac{d^2I}{dt^2}, \ldots, t\right).$$

Similarly, in view of (5.10), the coefficients of production are also functions of I and its time derivatives. Our equation (5.16) now becomes

$$(5.18) \qquad \frac{L}{K'} = n\left(I, \frac{dI}{dt}, \frac{d^2I}{dt^2}, \ldots, t\right).$$

---

* The integrated form of (5.11) is

$$b = b_0 + \int_0^t m'(I)\,dt.$$

Since $I = I(t)$, one can expand I in a Taylor series about $t = 0$ (if I and all its time derivatives are assumed to be continuous):

$$I = I(0) + t\,[dI(0)/dt] + \tfrac{1}{2}t^2[d^2I(0)/dt^2] + \ldots.$$

Inserting this expansion into $m'(I)$—a known function, by hypothesis—we can integrate the expression for b term by term to get (5.17).

The function $I(t)$, therefore, determines not only the coefficients of production and the organic composition of capital, but also the capital–labor ratio at every point of time.

Marx actually imposed additional restrictions upon the shape of the function $n(I, dI/dt, d^2I/dt^2, \ldots, t)$. According to his model, it is only during the first stage of accumulation (the "special phase") that the variable capital grows at the same rate as total capital. With the progress of capitalism a secular rise in the organic composition of capital takes place, and the variable capital falls relative to the total capital. In general, then,

> Since the demand for labour is determined not by the amount of capital as a whole, but by its variable constituent alone, that demand . . . falls relatively to the magnitude of the total capital, and at an accelerated rate, as this magnitude increases. With the growth of the total capital, its variable constituent or the labour incorporated in it also does increase, but in a constantly diminishing proportion.[40]

That is,

$$\frac{dn}{dK'} < 0\,, \tag{5.19}$$

$$\frac{d^2n}{dK'^2} < 0\,, \tag{5.20}$$

$$\frac{dL}{dK'} > 0\,, \tag{5.21}$$

and

$$\frac{d^2L}{dK'^2} < 0\,. \tag{5.22}$$

The first two equations are specific constraints upon the shape of the labor–capital ratio. Equation (5.21) says that the demand for labor is an increasing function of the rate of gross capital formation of the economy. However, since the ratio of variable to total capital diminishes with the growth of the capital stock, and since, in addition, demand for labor per unit of variable capital also drops, the demand for labor rises at a decreasing rate with the stock of capital [equation (5.22)].

Increase in Supply of Labor. The supply of labor increases with population growth, which Marx considered to be determined exogenously.[41] In addition, the ranks of the "would-be employed" are also enlarged by the technical changes in production, which are labor-displacing. These technological changes set free

> not only the labourers immediately turned out by the machines, but also their future substitutes in the rising generation, and the additional contingent, that with the usual extension of trade on the old basis would be regularly absorbed. . . . [As a result,] The demand for labour is not identical with increase of capital, nor the supply of labour with increase of the working class. . . . Capital works on both sides at the same time. If its accumulation, on the one hand, increases the demand for labour, it increases on the other the supply of labourers by the setting free of them, whilst at the same time the pressure of the unemployed compels those that are employed to furnish more labour, and therefore makes the supply of labour, to a certain extent, independent of the supply of labourers.[42]

The "Reserve Army" Concept. Hence, the normal condition of the labor market is one of excess supply, or of a "relative surplus-population." This relative surplus population, whose growth through time depends only in part upon the growth of population and whose existence Marx considered essential for capitalism,

> forms a disposable industrial reserve army, that belongs to capital quite as absolutely as if the latter had bred it at its own cost. Independently of the limits of the actual increase of population, it creates, for the changing needs of the self-expansion of capital, a mass of human material always ready for exploitation.[43]

The crucial function of this reserve army is to facilitate a rapid movement of capital among old branches of production and into new pursuits. It provides

> the possibility of throwing great masses of men suddenly on the decisive points without injury to the scale of production in other spheres. . . . [Hence it is] a necessity of modern industry. . . . The course characteristic of modern industry, *viz.,* a decennial cycle (interrupted by smaller oscillations), of periods of average activity, production at high pressure, crisis and stagnation, depends on the constant formation, the greater or less absorption, and the re-formation of the industrial reserve army of surplus population.[44]

The size of the reserve army also governs the magnitude of money wages through its influence upon the bargaining power of labor. Marx wrote: "Taking them as a whole, the general movements of wages are exclusively regulated by the expansion and contraction of the industrial reserve army, and these again correspond to the periodic changes of the industrial cycle."[45]

> The industrial reserve army, during the periods of stagnation and average prosperity, weighs down the active labour-army; during the periods of over-production and paroxysm, it holds its pretensions in check. Relative surplus-population is therefore the pivot upon which the law of demand and supply of labour works. It confines the field of action of this law within the limits absolutely convenient to the activity of exploitation and to the domination of capital.[46]

Wages therefore tend to fluctuate cyclically around the level of subsistence, which is defined as "the value of the means of subsistence necessary for the maintenance of the labourer."[47] It should be noted, however, that in Marx, as in Ricardo, the subsistence level is not a purely physiological quantity; rather, "there enters into the determination of the value of labour-power a historical and moral element."[48]

The magnitude of the reserve army increases with the size of the capital stock, for the larger the quantity of capital per worker the greater the productivity of labor, and therefore the smaller the number of workers employed to produce a given level of output.

> The fact that the means of production, and the productiveness of labour, increase more rapidly than the productive population, expresses itself, therefore, capitalistically in the inverse form that the labouring population always increases more rapidly than the conditions under which capital can employ this increase for its own self-expansion. . . . The greater the social wealth . . . the greater is the industrial reserve-army.[49]

In an expanding economy, then, the reserve army grows with time, and the bargaining power of labor becomes weaker as time goes on. "Accumulation of wealth at one pole, is therefore, at the same time accumulation of misery, agony of toil, slavery, ignorance, brutality, mental degradation, at the opposite pole, i.e., on the side of the class that produces its own product in the form of capital."[50]

Marx thus argued that with the progress of capitalism the position of the laborer grows progressively worse. In the *Communist Manifesto* (1848), for example, he wrote: "The modern laborer, on the contrary, instead of rising with the progress of industry, sinks deeper and deeper below the conditions of existence of his own class. He becomes a pauper, and pauperism develops more rapidly than population and wealth."[51] He states the case even more strongly in *Capital*:

> Within the capitalist system all methods for raising the social productiveness of labour are brought about at the cost of the individual labourer; all means for the development of production transform themselves into means of domination over, and exploitation of, the producers; they mutilate the labourer into a fragment of a man, degrade him to the level of an appendage of a machine, destroy every remnant of charm in his work and turn it into a hated toil; they estrange from him the intellectual potentialities of the labour-process in the same proportion as science is incorporated in it as an independent power; they distort the conditions under which he works, subject him during the labour-process to a despotism the more hateful for its meanness; they transform his life-time into working-time, and drag his wife and child beneath the wheels of the Juggernaut of capital. But all methods for the production of surplus value are at the same time methods of accumulation; and every extension of accumulation becomes again a means for the development of those methods. It follows therefore that in proportion as capital accumulates, the lot of the labourer, be his payment high or low, must grow worse.[52]

Critique of Marx's Predictions for the Working Classes. This prediction, of the progressive immiseration of the working class, has obviously not been borne out in the course of history. In industrial economies, the average real per capita income of the worker has risen, the relative share of labor has remained essentially unchanged, and working conditions have improved immensely since Marx's time. Therefore, the question naturally arises: "Is this prediction of Marx a rigorous consequence of his theoretical construct?" The answer, unfortunately, is not unique; it depends upon which of the several possible interpretations of Marx's writings one adopts.

If this doctrine of immiseration is taken to mean that either the total or the per capita real wages of the employed workers have a tendency to decline with economic development, it is inconsistent with the rest of Marx's theory. For, as pointed out above, the Marxian wage rate has a tendency to fluctuate around the level of subsistence during the entire process of growth, with the result that, on the average, the per capita wage rate remains constant. Furthermore, since the size of the active labor forces increases through time, the absolute magnitude of the wage bill increases. It is possible, of course, that Marx was really saying that the *relative* position of the workers deteriorates with progress.[53] Such an interpretation is more consistent with Marx's system, for, although the labor force expands with economic growth, it increases more slowly than the total capital stock. Since wages always remain at the subsistence level, the relative share of wages falls continually with the secular rise in the organic composition of capital. That is, a decline in labor's share of the economy's total product is actually implied by Marx's assumptions. But Marx appears to have meant more than this. Certainly, the tone of his statements on the immiseration of labor implies that he believed that the condition of the individual laborer would become significantly worse with time.[54]

Perhaps Marx was referring to the per capita income of the working class as a whole, including the unemployed. Since the proportion of the unemployed will increase with capital accumulation, whereas the wage rate stays close to subsistence, the real income of an average member of the working class will dwindle with industrial development. Perhaps, on the other hand, Marx's doctrine of progressive immiseration did not refer so much to the worker's material welfare as to his working conditions.[55] After all, with the increase of the size of the reserve army, the bargaining power of labor would be weakened, and the worker might well be faced with longer hours, more intensive and more routine types of work, and similar encroachments upon his rights. It appears that the combination of these two interpretations is quite consistent with Marx's writings in general.

Mathematical Recapitulation. Let us recapitulate for a moment. We have seen that the demand for labor is regulated by the rate of capital accumulation. Since the labor market is always in a state of excess supply, it is the demand for labor that determines the actual amount of labor employed in production. Therefore, we may substitute the demand for labor equation (5.14) into the rate of change of output equation (5.9). If, in addition, we use (5.10) and its integrated form to eliminate S and dS/dt from the equation, plus (5.14), (5.15), and (5.17) to express dL/dt in terms of K', dK'/dt, and I and its derivatives, and (5.13), (5.15), and (5.17) to express L in terms of K' and $I(t)$, we may rewrite (5.9) as

$$\frac{dY}{dt} = h'\left(K', \frac{dK'}{dt}, I, \frac{dI}{dt}, \frac{d^2I}{dt^2}, \ldots, t\right). \tag{5.23}$$

But, by definition, gross investment consists of net capital formation and depreciation (D). That is,

$$I = \frac{dK'}{dt} + D. \tag{5.24}$$

If we assume with Marx that the amount of depreciation is some increasing function of the size of the capital stock alone, (5.24) becomes

$$I = \frac{dK'}{dt} + a(K'). \tag{5.25}$$

Substituting (5.25) into (5.23), we get

$$\frac{dY}{dt} = h''\left(K', \frac{dK'}{dt}, \frac{d^2K'}{dt^2}, \ldots, t\right). \tag{5.26}$$

From this expression it is apparent that in the last analysis the clue to economic growth in Marx lies in the rate of capital accumulation. The limits to output expansion are set solely by the growth of productive capacity.

DETERMINANTS OF RATE OF CAPITAL ACCUMULATION

We must now inquire into the determinants of the rate of capital accumulation. Marx stated that the "magnitude of the capital accumulated clearly depends on the absolute magnitude of surplus-value."[56] It will be recalled that total income may be viewed as being composed of constant capital c, variable capital v, and surplus value s. The variable capital, or the wages fund, is spent entirely on consumer products. Similarly, a portion of revenue equal to the constant capital must be reinvested in order to maintain the economy's capital stock intact. The sole remaining source of funds available for net capital formation is then the surplus value, or profit. "Hence all the circumstances that determine the mass of surplus value, operate to determine the magnitude of the accumulation."[57]

In view of (5.13) we may write the surplus value as

$$s = (s/v)q_1L\,. \tag{5.27}$$

Therefore, as one increases the rate of exploitation of labor (s/v), the unit wage (q_1), or the number of labor units (L) used, the surplus value grows larger. Marx argued that the rate of exploitation of labor increases with rises in productivity: "But hand in hand with the increasing productivity of labour, goes . . . a higher rate of surplus value, even when the real wages are rising. The latter never rise proportionally to the productive power of labour."[58] And productivity increases with the size of the capital stock: "The more . . . capital increases by means of successive accumulations, the more does the sum of the value increase that is divided into consumption-fund and accumulation-fund."[59] In an expanding economy, then, the surplus value (or profit), together with the possibility for accumulation, increases progressively.

Of course, not all profit is reinvested. A portion must be set aside for consumption by the capitalists. "But it is by the owner of the surplus-value, by the capitalist alone, that the division is made."[60] It therefore becomes important to ask, "What guides the capitalist in his allocation of income among consumer and producer outlays?" The answer of the classical economist to this question is the rate of profit. Not so for Marx. As he sees it, the inducement to invest is independent of the rate of profit or the rate of interest, as the desire and necessity for investment are inherent in the psychological make-up of the capitalist and in the structure of society.

> Only as personified capital is the capitalist respectable. As such, he shares with the miser the passion for wealth as wealth. But that which in the miser is a mere idiosyncracy [*sic*], is, in the capitalist, the effect of the social mechanism, of which he is but one of the wheels. . . . It compels him to keep constantly extending his capital, in order to preserve it, but extend he cannot, except by means of progressive accumulation. . . . To accumulate, is to conquer the world of social wealth, to increase the mass of human beings exploited by him, and thus to extend both the direct and indirect sway of the capitalist.

The capitalist's motto must therefore be "Accumulate, accumulate! That is Moses and the Prophets."

The capitalist is consequently not too much interested in luxurious consumption for its own sake. In his eyes, "His own private consumption is a robbery perpetrated on accumulation." And, while he does exhibit "a conventional degree of prodigality," it is because this display of wealth provides him with a source of credit. Therefore the capitalist strives to minimize the leakage of revenue into consumption and does not engage in hoarding. His pattern of behavior is to "Save, save, i.e., reconvert the greatest possible portion of surplus-value, or surplus product into capital!" And since the amount of surplus value rises with time, so does the actual rate of capital accumulation. "The continual re-transformation of surplus-value into capital now appears in the shape of the increasing magnitude of the capital that enters into the process of production."[61]

Unfortunately, however, competition leads the capitalist to adopt more capital-intensive techniques, or, in Marx's terminology, to increase the organic composition of capital.

> *The numerical increase* of the capitals increases the *competition between the capitalists.* . . . One capitalist can drive another from the field and capture his capital only by selling more cheaply. In order to be able to sell more cheaply without ruining himself, he must produce more cheaply, that is, raise the productive power of labour as much as possible. But the productive power of labour is raised, above all, by a *greater division of labour,* by a more universal introduction and continual improvement of *machinery.* . . . However, the *privileged position* of our capitalist is not of long duration; other competing capitalists introduce the same machines, the same division of labour, introduce them on a larger scale, and this introduction will become so general that the price . . . is *reduced* not only *below its old, but below its new cost of production.* The capitalists find themselves, therefore, in the same position relative to one another as *before* the introduction of the new means of production. . . . On the basis of this new cost of production, the same game begins again. More division of labour, more machinery, enlarged scale of exploitation of machinery and division of labour. And again competition brings the same counter-action against this result.[62]

Theory of Declining Rate of Profit. As capital expands, the rate of profit declines. Marx deduced this theorem of a declining rate of profit by means of an identity; by definition, the rate of profit equals the rate of return on advanced capital.[63] That is,

$$(5.28) \qquad r = \frac{s}{v + c} = \frac{s/v}{1 + c/v}.$$

Therefore, the rate of profit rises with the rate of exploitation of labor $(s/v = e)$ and falls with the organic composition of capital $(c/v = b)$. Using this new notation for convenience, we see that (5.28) becomes

$$(5.29) \qquad r = \frac{e}{1 + b}.$$

Differentiating with respect to time, we have

$$(5.30) \qquad \frac{dr}{dt} = \frac{1}{1 + b}\frac{de}{dt} - \frac{e}{(1 + b)^2}\frac{db}{dt},$$

or

$$(5.31) \qquad \frac{dr}{dt} = \frac{1}{1 + b}\left[\frac{de}{dt} - r\frac{db}{dt}\right].$$

If we assume that the rate of profit is less than 100 per cent, it is evident that so long as the rate of exploitation of labor increases more rapidly than the organic composition of capital, the rate of profit will grow with time. On the other hand, whenever the rate of exploitation does not keep pace with the organic composition of capital, it does *not* follow from (5.31) that the rate of profit will fall. In order for this latter conclusion to be valid, the rate of growth of the organic composition of capital must be so rapid that even when it is multiplied by the rate of return (which we have assumed to be less than one) the product will exceed the corresponding increment in the rate of exploitation.

Marx's argument was that with a constant rate of exploitation of labor and an increasing amount of capital per man the rate of profit would shrink.[64] However, these two assumptions are mutually inconsistent, unless real wages are allowed to rise secularly (which Marx denied).[65] For an increase in the organic composition of capital implies a rise in the productivity of labor, which must be reflected either in a wage hike or in a higher rate of exploitation. In order to devise a rigorous proof of a universal tendency toward a declining rate of return, then, one must demonstrate that the percentage increase in total output is less than the percentage increase in invested capital,* at the same time allowing for the fact that technology improves with capital accumulation.[66] Since Marx failed to prove this (or an equivalent theorem), and since history seems actually to refute the theorem as here stated, Marx's deduction of a secular decrease in the rate of profit remains singularly unconvincing.

THE MARXIAN DYNAMIC PROCESS

In any case, since investment is independent of the rate of profit, a declining rate fails to check accumulation. Indeed, since we have the law that "the fall in the rate of profit due to the development of the productive powers is accompanied by an increase in the mass of profit,"[67] it follows that a "fall in the rate of profit and a hastening of accumulation are in so far only different expressions of the same process as both of them indicate the development of the productive power."[68] Concomitant with the acceleration of capital accumulation we have also an intensification of competition among capitalists, caused, at least in part, by the fall in the rate of profit.[69] In response to this competitive struggle, capitalists enhance the rate at which they substitute capital equipment for labor.

> As a result, the size of the reserve army expands faster. Thus, the fall in prices and the competitive struggle would have given to every capitalist an impulse to raise the individual value of his total product above its average value by means of new machines, new and improved working methods, new combinations, which means, to increase the productive power of a certain quantity of labor, to lower the proportion of the variable to the constant capital, and thereby to release some laborers, in short, to create an artificial overpopulation.[70]

---

* By definition: (1) $Y = v + c + s$ or (2) $Y/(v+c) = 1 + s/(v+c) = 1 + r$. Differentiating and performing a little algebra, we get

$$\frac{dY/dt}{Y} - \frac{1}{v+c}\frac{d(v+c)}{dt} = \frac{1}{1+r}\frac{dr}{dt}.$$

Also, among industrial capitalists who attempt to take advantage of external economies, there is a movement toward increasing concentration and centralization: "A fall in the rate of profit hastens the concentration of capital and its centralisation through the expropriation of the smaller capitalists, the expropriation of the last survivors of the direct producers who still have anything to give up."[71] The growth of monopolistic and oligopolistic forms of industrial organization accelerates the rate of capital accumulation and the rise in the organic composition of capital, and therefore drives the rate of profit down even faster. "The battle of competition is fought by cheapening of commodities. The cheapness of commodities depends, *caeteris paribus,* on the productiveness of labour, and this again on the scale of production. Therefore, the larger capitals beat the smaller."[72]

The centralization of capital is speeded up by the intervention of the credit system, which

> transforms itself into an immense social mechanism for the centralisation of capitals. . . . At the same time the progress of accumulation increases the matter subject to centralisation, that is, the individual capitals, while the expansion of capitalist production creates the social demand here, the technical requirements there, for those gigantic industrial enterprises, which depend for their realisation on a previous centralisation of capitals.[73]

Indeed, observed Marx,

> the world would still be without railroads if it had been obliged to wait until accumulation should have enabled a few individual capitals to undertake the construction of a railroad. . . . Centralisation, by thus accelerating and intensifying the effects of accumulation, extends and hastens at the same time the revolutions in the technical composition of capital, which increase its constant part at the expense of its variable part and thereby reduce the relative demand for labor.[74]

The reserve army grows; the rate of profit falls. But total profit expands. Competition among capitalists becomes intensified. As a result, technological progress, the substitution of capital for labor, and the centralization of industrial capital proceed at an accelerated pace. "For the rest, the same vicious circle would be described once more under expanded conditions of production, in an expanded market, and with increased productive forces."[75] In this manner the capitalist economy races toward its doom.

Internal Contradictions in Capitalism. Inherent in capitalist systems are certain internal contradictions, which stem from the very nature of capitalist production and of the capitalist spirit. The most serious internal contradictions of the system are that production is motivated primarily by the desire to accumulate more capital rather than by social needs and wants,[76] and that the ownership and control of the means of production are in private (rather than public) hands.[77] These internal contradictions lead to increasingly severe economic maladjustments.

This point will become clearer as we explore Marx's reasoning. Assume that in view of the rise in capital per worker, the rate of profit is a decreasing function of the total capital stock, even when the effects of technological progress are included. Then, since accumulation is a capitalistic end in and of itself, it is not slowed down by the fall in the rate of profit. The failure of the economy to adjust the rate of investment to the rate of profit leads to ruthless competition among capitalists. In an effort to escape the ghost of a declining profit rate, they substitute capital for labor and attempt to increase their scale of output. This rise in the organic composition of capital enlarges the reserve army of the unemployed, drives down the share of wages in total output, and reduces the average income of the members of the working class taken as a whole. The movement of centralization leads to the expropriation of some capitalists by others and, by permitting the exploitation of ever more capital-intensive technology, contributes to the growth of the reserve army. The rate of profit declines, but total profits rise, since (by assumption) the fall in the average rate of profits is more than compensated for by the rise in total capital employed in production. Therefore, the amount of capital-seeking investment outlets expands, and the process now repeats itself on a larger scale.

Cyclical Movements. In addition, the internal contradictions of the system manifest themselves also in periodic economic crises. These disturbances "are always but momentary and forcible solutions of the existing contradictions, violent eruptions, which restore the disturbed equilibrium for a while."[78] Their origin is not unique; in fact, Marx presented us with the germs of several different theories of the evolution of cyclical fluctuations. First of all, there is the theory of crises developed in the second volume of *Capital,* which is related to the interruption of the circular flow of payments in the economy by the periodic hoarding and dishoarding of investment funds. This type of cycle can arise regardless of whether net investment takes place (Marx's simple reproduction scheme) or not (Marx's expanded reproduction).[79]

Consider first the case of simple reproduction. In such an economy the entire output is divided between current consumption, on the one hand, and the replacement of worn-out capital equipment, on the other. However, since, in a monetary economy, depreciation funds are accumulated in the form of cash, amortization funds in any one year may exceed, equal, or fall short of actual replacement expenditures. When depreciation allowances are larger than such spending, hoards increase and we have a slump. In the opposite case we have a boom.

Similarly, in an expanding economy: "Balance can be maintained only on the assumption that the value of the one-sided purchases and one-sided sales is the same"; but a balance is "an accident under the crude conditions of this [capitalist] production."[80] In general, savings and investment will not be equal, implying the possibility of crises, since the return to the circular flow of the constant capital (c) and of the surplus value (s) is not automatic. Portions of either of these elements may be accumulated temporarily in the form of cash, before reconversion into capital goods. Whenever this occurs, saving exceeds investment and a crisis results. Since the ratio of ($s + c$) to total output goes up with the growth of the economy, the relative magnitude of the volatile component of income will increase with time, and the economy can anticipate increasingly severe cyclical fluctuations.

This theory of business cycles, which is based upon the repudiation of Say's Law, is an internally consistent one and sounds, indeed, quite Keynesian in nature. Unlike Keynes, however, Marx did not relate the rate of accumulation or dissipation of money in hoards to the level of the rate of interest. The only reasons Marx advanced for not converting investment funds into investment products immediately are (1) the lumpiness of investment, which requires the accumulation of sizable sums before capital equipment can be purchased; and (2) the non-availability on the market of the precise items of productive capital desired by the investor.[81] Marx's hoard thus consists only of funds accumulated with Keynes's investment motive in mind, and is therefore normally smaller than the Keynesian one.

In the third volume of *Capital,* Marx attempted to devise a theory of cyclical fluctuations within the framework of a Say's Law economy.[82] According to this theory, the growth of the economy leads to a contradiction between the narrow basis of consumption on the one hand and the ever-expanding productive powers of society[83] on the other. As the economy matures, the share of wages in total output drops, whereas the share of profits increases. Also, the entire wage income, plus a portion of profit income is spent on consumption goods. But since the relative share of wages declines and capitalist consumption does not rise as fast as capitalist income,[84] the proportion of aggregate demand that is directed toward consumer products declines with time. Therefore, a growing economy generates an increasing gap between aggregate supply on the one hand and consumption demand on the other.

As a cyclical theory, however, this argument is fallacious. If, as Marx assumed, investment demand always suffices to fill the gap,[85] a cycle will not emerge, no matter how depressed the consumption level might be. For a cycle to develop, investment must be made to fluctuate, sometimes undershooting and sometimes exceeding the difference between consumer demand and total output. This could occur in two ways: (1) if the rate of investment were tied to the rate of profit, and if the profit rate were permitted to fluctuate with the level of consumption; or (2) if the demand for capital goods varies directly with the output of consumer goods industries through an accelerator mechanism. In either case, cyclical fluctuations of increasing severity would result as the economy expands, since, with growth, the share of wages income (and hence of consumption expenditures) progressively declines. In this way we could construct within the Marxian framework a consistent theory of progressively severe cyclical movements; however, we could no longer assume that the rate of investment is independent of the inducement to invest.

From his analysis of the internal contradictions of the capitalist system, Marx concluded:

> *The real barrier of capitalist production is capital itself*. It is the fact that capital and its self-expansion appear as the starting and closing point, as the motive and aim of production; that production

> is merely production for *capital,* and not vice versa, the means of production mere means for an ever expanding system of the life process for the benefit of the *society* of producers. The barriers, within which the preservation and self-expansion of the value of capital resting on the expropriation and pauperisation of the great mass of producers can alone move, these barriers come continually in collision with the methods of production, which capital must employ for its purposes, and which steer straight toward an unrestricted extension of production, toward production for its own self, toward an unconditional development of the productive forces of society. The means, this unconditional development of the productive forces of society, comes continually into conflict with the limited end, the self-expansion of the existing capital. Thus, while the capitalist mode of production is one of the historical means by which the material forces of production are developed and the world-market required for them created, it is at the same time in continual conflict with this historical task and the conditions of social production corresponding to it.[86]

At this stage of development, the productive forces at the disposal of society "no longer tend to further the development of the conditions of bourgeois property; on the contrary, they have become too powerful for these conditions by which they are fettered." The result is predictable: "The development of modern industry . . . cuts from under its feet the very foundations on which the bourgeoisie produces and appropriates products. What the bourgeoisie therefore produces, above all, are its own gravediggers. Its fall and the victory of the proletariat are equally inevitable."[87] Communism replaces capitalism.

Summary of Marx's Theory of Economic Development. Before inquiring into the empirical and theoretical validity of Marx's doctrines about the historical evolution of a capitalist economy, let us pause to summarize his analysis of economic development. It is apparent from equation (5.26) that once the initial capital stock (K'_0) is given, the progress of the system is regulated by the course of capital accumulation. But the rate of capital accumulation itself depends upon the distribution of income among wage earners and profit takers. Moreover, since the trend of wages is set at subsistence, the share of wages in total output depends upon the employment of labor; and the employment of labor is determined by the demand for labor, which, in turn, is limited by the available capacity, given the development of technical knowledge [see (5.18)]. The level of technique is also governed by the history of capital accumulation [equation (5.10)]; therefore the current rate of investment can be expressed in terms of the historical path of capital accumulation, i.e.,

$$\frac{dK'}{dt} = F\left(K', \frac{dK'}{dt}, \frac{d^2K'}{dt^2}, \ldots, t\right), \tag{5.29}$$

where the precise form of F can be derived from the equations given earlier in this chapter. Since the only independent variables in (5.29) are the size of the capital stock and all its time derivatives, this equation can be solved, in principle, to yield an explicit solution for K' as a function of time. Thus the only factors that can influence the time path of the capital stock are the functional form of (5.29) and the initial state of the economy. Given these, which define the economy completely, the entire history of capital accumulation follows. This is not really a surprising conclusion; after all, what other result should one expect from a system in which the supply of labor, technological and organizational knowledge, and the structure of society are all perfectly adapted to the requirements of production, and from a society, moreover, in which capital accumulation proceeds as fast as possible?

The solution to (5.29) may be written in terms of the initial conditions of the economy and of its structural parameters as

$$K' = K'(K'_0, L_0, S_0, U_0; t; \alpha_1, \ldots, \alpha_N). \tag{5.30}$$

Since

$$Y = Y_0 + \int_0^t \left(\frac{dY}{dt}\right) dt, \tag{5.31}$$

we can use (5.26) and (5.30) to write down an explicit expression for the time path of output

$$Y = Y(K'_0, L_0, S_0, U_0; t; \alpha_1, \ldots, \alpha_N). \tag{5.32}$$

We see, then, that the evolution of a Marxian economy is uniquely determined by the initial conditions of the system and its structural parameters. There are no degrees of freedom in this system. Once the economy has started, its course is fixed. The future development of the society (economic and otherwise) will proceed in a predictable manner along an inescapable path.

With the passage of time, the economy's capital stock, and hence its level of output, expand. But, according to Marx, this is not an unmitigated blessing. As the economy progresses, the distribution of income between workers and capitalists becomes more and more unequal. Technological unemployment mounts. The rate of profit declines, generating a fierce competitive struggle among capitalists and leading to a further concentration of ownership of the means of production. An increasingly smaller share of total output is devoted to the production of consumer goods. Cyclical fluctuations become increasingly more severe. Finally, as the structural maladjustments in the economy mount, the system collapses. And the ultimate breakdown is occasioned by the very increase in wealth and income which it has brought about.

MARX'S THEORY OF UNDERDEVELOPMENT

In view of the fact that Marx considered this sequence inevitable, how can he account for the major underdeveloped portions of the world? Since his system is purely endogenous in nature, his explanation of this phenomenon is based upon adverse initial conditions and/or structural parameters. In the case of India, for example, he wrote:

> Climate and territorial conditions, especially the vast tracts of desert . . . [made] artificial irrigation by canals and waterworks the basis of Oriental agriculture. . . . This prime necessity of an economical and common use of water, which, in the Occident, drove private enterprise to voluntary association, as in Flanders and Italy, necessitated in the Orient, where civilisation was too low and the territorial extent too vast to call into life voluntary association, the interference of the centralising power of Government.[88]

The people were both "dispersed . . . over the surface of the country, and agglomerated in small centres by the domestic union of agricultural and manufacturing pursuits—these two circumstances had brought about, since the remotest times, a social system of particular features—the so called VILLAGE-SYSTEM."[89] Unfortunately, "These little communities transformed a self-developing social state into never-changing natural destiny."[90] In this manner, a particular combination of S_0 and N_0 led to the growth of an institutional structure (U) which was incompatible with the further development of technology. The VILLAGE-

SYSTEM in fact prevented the establishment of a feudal economy and thereby precluded the emergence of pre-capitalist economic forms. As a result, the economic and social system in India became stagnant.

Is there then any hope for future economic development in India? Since economic development can occur as a result of the imposition of strong exogenous shocks, Marx believed that there was. He visualized great prospects for India, solely as a result of British colonization.[91] "British steam and science uprooted, over the whole surface of Hindustan, the union between agricultural and manufacturing industry."[92] It had "broken down the entire framework of Indian society, without any symptoms of reconstitution yet appearing."[93] His hope was that the introduction of modern industrial techniques of production would precipitate in India the emergence of capitalism and would thereby "create the material basis of the new world."[94] (He was later disenchanted with the results of British colonization.) One can see, then, that for Marx, underdevelopment is the consequence of a particular adverse combination of initial conditions and structural parameters, which results in economic and social stagnation. Development can occur only as a result of an exogenous shock, the essential effect of which is to change the initial conditions in such a way that self-sustained growth takes place.

CRITIQUE OF MARX'S THEORY

We are finally in a position to inquire into the validity of Marx's theory of capitalist development. We shall do this from two points of view. First, we shall examine the internal consistency of Marx's theoretical framework, given his postulates.* Next, we shall investigate to what extent his generalizations have been borne out by subsequent economic and social developments.

From a theoretical standpoint, Marx's demonstration that an increase in the organic composition of capital leads to a declining rate of profit is questionable. As already pointed out, any rise in the organic composition of capital implies not only an increase in the productivity of labor but changes in technology. Both of these effects tend to counteract the pressures pushing the rate of profit downward. In the event

* As indicated at the beginning of this chapter, we shall not concern ourselves with the applicability of his basic assumptions.

that the rate of profit does not fall as the organic composition of capital rises, competition among capitalists need not intensify with capital accumulation, and innovations need no longer be purely labor-displacing. As a result, the reserve army need not grow secularly, and the share of wages in total output need not decline.

Marx's second logical error is connected with industrial growth. It is true that the possibility of external economies may lead to a growth in the size of the average firm, but it does not necessarily imply a rise in the degree of concentration of industry. In an expanding economy, the size of the industry may keep pace with the growth in the size of the efficient firm, or even outrun it. Finally, since the share of wages in aggregate income need not drop with economic development, neither must the share of consumption. Therefore cyclical fluctuations need not become increasingly severe. Marx's proof of the internal contradictions of the capitalist system would thus appear *not* to be a direct consequence of his hypotheses.

The empirical evidence, too, does not support Marx's theoretical predictions. For example, the real wages of workers have not sunk to a miserably low level, but instead have risen consistently in the industrial capitalist world.[95] The share of wages in total output has not fallen; rather it has remained approximately constant.[96] The capital intensity of production has increased somewhat, as Marx predicted, even in the face of the drastic shift in the composition of output toward tertiary industries.[97] But in spite of this, the rate of capital accumulation has been so rapid that the structural unemployment of the labor force has not increased very markedly (although it has risen slightly).[98] The capital–output ratio has declined slightly, implying a *rise* in the average productivity of capital, most probably due to the abundance of innovating activity.[99] This rise has been sufficient for both capital accumulation and an increase in real wages to take place simultaneously. Contrary to Marx's expectations, industrial concentration has increased very little (if at all) since the turn of the century.[100] Similarly, the size distribution of income has not varied significantly; if anything, inequality has been reduced somewhat.[101] Moreover, the amplitude of cyclical fluctuations has not increased secularly. Finally, in addition to all this statistical evidence, "Current experience suggests that socialism is not a stage beyond capitalism but a substitute for it. . . . This makes a drastic reconsideration of Marx's central hypothesis necessary.[102]

In spite of these deficiencies in long-term prediction, however, Marx's analysis of economic growth and development constitutes a tremendous intellectual achievement. No reader of Marx can fail to be struck by the scope and power of his analysis. Indeed, his theories have a breadth rarely encountered among economists, since he postulated that the entire legal, institutional, cultural, and social life of a community is determined by the character of its economic activities. While his specific conclusions apparently have not been borne out in the course of history, his framework of analysis can still be extremely useful, provided (and this is essential) that it is applied flexibly. For example, his system lends itself quite easily to an investigation of the relationship between the character of technological change, the distribution of income through time, capital accumulation, and economic growth.[103]

Marx's scheme for expanded reproduction provides a basis for a useful analysis of the interrelation between long-run development, savings, and investment as monetary and real flows, a line of study which was later taken up independently by both Harrod[104] and Domar.[105] The inherently dynamic nature of Marx's models provides an excellent example of the power and importance of dynamic analysis. Finally, Marx's emphasis on the relationships between disequilibrium systems and internally generated growth and between equilibrium systems and stagnation has recently been reformulated and re-emphasized by Leibenstein,[106] and offers a useful approach to the problems of underdevelopment. In short, as pointed out by Mrs. Robinson: "If Marx had been studied as a serious economist, instead of being treated on the one hand as an infallible oracle and on the other as a butt for cheap epigrams, he would have saved us all a great deal of time.[107]

SIX

SCHUMPETER

THE MAIN PROBLEM to which Joseph A. Schumpeter addressed himself throughout his work was how to explain the process of economic development. His analysis of the origin, operation, and evolution of capitalism constitutes the most important neo-classical contribution to an understanding of the dynamics of capitalist systems. In the literature on economic development, Schumpeter's name has become linked to the twin notions of "innovation" and "entrepreneur." In view of the corporate nature of the innovating process in large-scale enterprise today,[1] the explanatory value of the entrepreneurial hypothesis for advanced capitalist economies is open to question; Schumpeter's theory, however, still offers penetrating insights into the reasons for the stagnation of underdeveloped economies.

PROCESS OF PRODUCTION

The process of production was characterized by Schumpeter as a "combination of productive forces," whose end results are the products; these forces "comprise partly material, partly immaterial things."[2] On the material level, we have the original factors of production, labor and land, from which all goods come. The producer goods, too, "are, on the one hand, only the embodiment of those two original production goods, on the other 'potential' consumption goods."[3] Whereas Schumpeter did not consider producer goods to be independent factors of production, he did not deny that their services participate in manufacturing activity. Thus he wrote:

> In successive productive processes or combinations each good matures into a consumption good through the addition of other goods . . . with the help of such additions it makes its way to the consumer just as a stream, helped by inflowing rivulets of water, breaks its way through the rock even more deeply into the earth.[4]

On the intangible plane, "technical facts" and the "facts of social organization"[5] also serve to condition the nature and level of economic activity. Although for static analysis we can take these two forces of production as given,[6] Schumpeter assigned a vital role to technical and social factors in economic dynamics.[7]

Schumpeter's production function may be written in our general form

$$Y = f(K, N, L, S, U)\,. \tag{6.1}$$

In this expression, K stands for the Schumpeterian concept of "produced means of production," not for his notion of "capital." This distinction is vital, since, as we shall see later, Schumpeter imparted to the term "capital" a meaning quite different from the usual one.

The rate of change of economic activity may then be derived from (6.1), as before, to yield

$$\frac{dY}{dt} = \frac{\partial f}{\partial K}\frac{dK}{dt} + \frac{\partial f}{\partial L}\frac{dL}{dt} + \frac{\partial f}{\partial N}\frac{dN}{dt} + \frac{\partial f}{\partial S}\frac{dS}{dt} + \frac{\partial f}{\partial U}\frac{dU}{dt}. \tag{6.2}$$

Thus the growth of output depends upon the rate of change of the productive factors, the rate of change of technology, and the rate of change of the socio-cultural environment. However, Schumpeter did not consider all these factors to be equally important contributors to the rate of the economy's growth. He felt, rather, that changes in the supply of the productive factors can bring about only a gradual evolution of the economic system, and hence that the integrated effect of changes in factor availability upon the historical rise in income of Western economies is dwarfed by comparison with the impact of technological and social change. Thus he wrote: "Increase in productive resources might at first sight appear to be the obvious prime mover in the process of internal economic change. Physical environment being taken as constant . . . that increase resolves itself into increase of population and the increase in the stock of producers' goods."[8] However:

> The mere growth of the economy, as shown by the growth of population and wealth . . . calls forth no qualitatively new phenomena, but only processes of adaptation of the same kind as changes in the

> natural data. . . . [Besides,] these changes are small per annum and therefore do not stand in the way of the applicability of the "static" method.[9]

On the other hand: "Different methods of employment (of existing factor supplies), and not savings and increases in the available quantity of labor, have changed the face of the economic world in the last fifty years."[10]

DYNAMIC EVOLUTION OF AN ECONOMY

In view of these considerations, Schumpeter felt that it would be desirable to distinguish between two classes of influences upon the dynamic evolution of an economy: (1) the effects of changes in factor availabilities [the first three terms of (6.2)], which he called the "growth" component; and (2) the effects of technological and social change [the last two terms of (6.2)], which he referred to as "development" or "evolution."

Schumpeter defined these two classes of factors as follows:

> We shall designate by the term (positive or negative) Growth changes in population . . . and in the sum total of savings plus accumulations corrected for variation in the purchasing power . . . of the monetary unit. That term is to emphasize not only that variation in both these variables is continuous in the mathematical sense . . . but also that it occurs at a rate which changes but slowly.[11]

On the other hand:

> Development in our sense is a distinct phenomenon, entirely foreign to what may be observed in the circular flow or in the tendency towards equilibrium. It is spontaneous and discontinuous change in the channels of the flow, disturbance of equilibrium, which forever alters and displaces the equilibrium state previously existing. Our theory of development is nothing but a treatment of this phenomenon and the processes incident to it.

In other words, development is "that kind of change arising from within the system *which so displaces its equilibrium point that the new one cannot be reached from the old one by infinitesimal steps.* Add successively as many mail coaches as you please, and you will never get a railway thereby."[12]

Let us first look at the growth component of economic change. As pointed out earlier, this component represents the contribution of variations in the use of productive factors to changes in the total output of the economy. Since land was taken by Schumpeter to be constant,[13] we may write that

$$dN/dt = 0 \,. \tag{6.3}$$

The growth component therefore includes only the effects of changes in population and of increases in producer goods.

For Schumpeter population growth was exogenously determined. He felt that there does not exist a unique *a priori* relationship between changes in population and variations in the flow of goods and services.[14] Despite this, however, he considered population-induced increases in output to be part of the "growth" term rather than part of the "development" component. The growth of population is a slow process, which is not subject to violent independent fluctuations.[15] Hence, "On the whole it is much more correct to say that population grows slowly up to the possibilities of any economic environment than that it has any tendency to outgrow it and to become thereby an independent cause of change."[16] Therefore, "It seemed convenient for our purpose, although it would be inadequate for others, to look upon an increase in population as an environmental change conditioning certain phenomena."[17]

In mathematical terms, Schumpeter's views on population growth may be summarized as

$$L = L(t) \,. \tag{6.4}$$

Similarly, increases in producer goods, which ordinarily result from a positive rate of net savings,[18] also belong in the "growth" portion of total output. "Long time changes in the rate of savings come about by truly infinitesimal steps. . . . Autonomously, abrupt changes in the rate of savings hardly ever occur."[19] Moreover, Schumpeter felt that in the long run the economy tends to adapt itself to any rate of savings undertaken by the community. He argued that savings, too, are rarely an independent cause of change.

> We start from competitive equilibrium, although extension to the imperfectly competitive case would not present any difficulties. Now, that equilibrium is incessantly disturbed by the flow of new savings which are being offered to the firm. If, however, the system is

> adapted to the actual rate of savings—an assumption which is not only reasonable under the circumstances of this model, but also much nearer the truth in reality than devotees of oversaving theories are in the habit of admitting—this disturbance will be currently absorbed; for, as long as saving goes on at all, each installment will depress the rate of interest to the extent required to create its own investment opportunity.[20]

But, more important still, the historical increase in the stock of producer goods owes its quantitative magnitude primarily to those dynamic elements which are largely absent in a smoothly expanding economy.

> Whatever definition of saving the reader adopts, it is clear that most of its sources, as well as most of the motives for it, would be absent in a stationary state. If we take up any of the familiar attempts at estimating statistically the amount of saving done in any country at any time, we see immediately that the bulk of it, whether done within the sphere of business or the sphere of households, flows from revenues or elements of revenues which would not exist at all in a stationary state, namely from profits, or from other incomes created or swelled by previous economic change. As to motives, it is equally obvious that most of them arise out of situations incident to economic change . . . its quantitative importance would be exceedingly small . . . if the economic process in any way approximated the equilibrium picture: Saving would be a "trickle."[21]

Hence the major part of savings and accumulation can be attributed to profits.

But "without development there is no profit, without profit no development."[22] In the circular flow, the value of the product is exactly equal to the value of the means of production incorporated in it. Hence there are no profits. If new techniques of production are employed to manufacture a certain product, or if a new product is introduced, profits can arise. Then the value of the product must be compared to the value that could have been generated by employing the same doses of the means of production *using the old techniques*. If the value of the means of production obtained is lower than the value of the product, profits are generated. The source of profits, then, is the carrying out of new combinations of the factors of production (i.e., technological change). And, since "for the capitalist system it must be added further that without profit there would be no accumulation of wealth,"[23] it is the changes in the fund of *applied* technical knowledge that are responsible for changes in the stock of producer goods. Hence we may write that for Schumpeter a good approximation to reality is

$$(6.5) \qquad \frac{dK}{dt} = k\left(\frac{dS}{dt}\right).$$

In other words, the rate of capital accumulation is tied to the rate of technological change, and rises and falls with it. Hence, "growth, but especially saving, owes its actual quantitative importance to another factor of change without which its *modus operandi* in the capitalist world cannot be understood."[24]

Before we turn to a detailed examination of this factor, however, let us look briefly at the second component of the "development" term, the change in socio-cultural environment. With respect to the social factors, Schumpeter subscribed to Marx's materialistic interpretation of history. He wrote:

> Because of this fundamental dependence of the economic aspect of things on everything else, it is not possible to explain *economic* change by previous *economic* conditions alone. For the economic state of a people does not emerge simply from the preceding economic conditions, but only from the preceding total situation. The expository and analytical difficulties which arise from this are very much diminished, practically if not in principle, by the facts which form the basis of economic interpretation of history; without being compelled to take a stand for or against this view, we can state that the economic world is relatively autonomous because it takes up such a great part of a nation's life, and forms or conditions a great part of the remainder.[25]

Hence in Schumpeter,*

$$(6.6) \qquad dU/dt = U(K, L, N, S, U).$$

Since equation (6.5) can be integrated to give K as a function of S and all its time derivatives [see footnote, p. 73], and since L is exogenous [equation (6.4)] and N fixed [equation (6.3)], equation (6.6) is a differential equation relating the two dependent variables, S and U, to

* An equation analogous to (6.6) can obviously be inferred from the same quotation for each of the other economic variables. However, since Schumpeter imposes more specific restrictions upon the other variables of the system, we do not choose to discuss them in the same way as U.

the independent variable, time. Similarly, the rate of change of output [equation (6.2)] can be written as

$$(6.7) \qquad \frac{dY}{dt} = g\left(S, \frac{dS}{dt}, \frac{d^2S}{dt^2}, \ldots; U, t\right).$$

Therefore, if we can evaluate the technological index S as a function of time, we can solve (6.6) to get U as a function of time and we can substitute into (6.7) to obtain the time path of output. Ultimately, then, the rate of growth of output depends (1) upon the exogenously determined rate of population expansion, which fixes the trend of economic growth, and (2) upon the history of technological progress. Let us first inquire into the influence of technology on the development component.

INFLUENCE OF TECHNOLOGY ON DEVELOPMENT

Actually, for Schumpeter, economic development is synonymous with discontinuous technological change. Thus he wrote:

> In so far as the "new combination" [of the material forces of production] may in time grow out of the old by continuous adjustment in small steps, there is certainly change, possibly growth, but neither a new phenomenon nor development in our sense. In so far as this is not the case, and the new combinations appear discontinuously, then the phenomenon characterizing development emerges. For reasons of expository convenience, henceforth, we shall only mean the latter case when we speak of new combinations of productive means. Development in our sense is then defined by the carrying out of new combinations.[26]

The process of development can be generated by five different classes of events:[27] (1) it can arise from the introduction of a new commodity; (2) it can be the result of a new method of production; (3) it can be the consequence of the opening up of a new market; (4) it can be due to the conquest of a new source of supply of raw materials; or (5) it can emerge because of a change in the organization of any industry. All these cases involve a different employment of the production factors, and hence, by definition, they constitute "development."

But development does not arise spontaneously. It must be actively promoted by some agency within the system. Schumpeter called the agent whose function is to introduce new combinations of the factors of production an "entrepreneur," and what he creates is known as "enterprise" or "innovation."[28]

NATURE OF THE ENTREPRENEUR

The sole distinguishing characteristic of the entrepreneur is that he is an innovator. By forcing the means of production into new channels, he provides the economic leadership that spearheads discontinuous dynamic change. The pure entrepreneur is not necessarily the head of a business, and may not even be permanently associated with a particular firm.[29] Although he may assume managerial functions, these activities do not define his work as entrepreneurial in character.[30] That is, the entrepreneur must not be confused with the manager of an enterprise. Similarly, while the entrepreneur may be either an inventor or a capitalist (or both), he will perform these functions merely by coincidence rather than by the inherent logic of his role.[31] By nature he is neither a technician nor a financier; he is an innovator, no more and no less. Since being an entrepreneur is neither a profession nor a permanent occupation, entrepreneurs do not constitute a social class like capitalists or workers.[32]

Psychologically, entrepreneurs are not motivated solely by the desire for profit.

> First of all, there is the dream and the will to found a private kingdom, usually, though not necessarily, also a dynasty. . . . Then there is the will to conquer; the impulse to fight, to prove oneself superior to others, to succeed for the sake, not of the fruits of success, but of success itself. . . . Finally, there is the joy of creating, of getting things done, or simply of exercising one's energy and ingenuity.[33]

Thus, like the Marxian capitalist, who accumulates for the sake of accumulation, the Schumpeterian innovator innovates, at least in part, for the sake of innovating.

The nature and activities of the entrepreneur are conditioned by the socio-cultural environment in which he operates. Indeed, capitalist rationality and bourgeois institutions are so essential to successful entrepreneurship that they may be said to constitute preconditions for the flourishing of entrepreneurial activity. The emergence of capitalism gave rise to the spirit of individual rationalism, and hence to the mental attitudes conducive to scientific investigation.[34] It turned "the unit of money into a tool of rational cost-profit calculations, of which the towering monument is double-entry bookkeeping."[35] And by breaking up feudal institutions, capitalism also created the social space for a new class, whose distinction is based only upon its economic achievements. Therefore, "It is . . . quite wrong . . . to say, as many economists do, that capitalist enterprise was one, and technological progress a second, distinct factor in the observed development of output; they were essentially one and the same thing or, as we may also put it, the former was the propelling force of the latter."[36]

In order to perform his economic function the entrepreneur requires two things. First of all, there must exist the technical knowledge that enables him to produce new products or to combine factors in a different manner. This, Schumpeter felt, poses no problem, for at any point of time there exists a reservoir of unused technical inventions which the would-be entrepreneur can tap. Therefore, "It is no part of his function to 'find' or to 'create' new possibilities. They are always present, abundantly accumulated by all sorts of people."[37]

Meaning of Capital. Second, since the introduction of innovations presupposes the diversion of the means of production from existing channels into new processes, the entrepreneur must also possess the "power of disposal" over the factors of production. The necessary command over productive factors is provided by monetary claims, in the form of credit. It is these newly created forms of purchasing power which constitute "capital" in Schumpeter's sense: "We shall define capital, then, as that sum of means of payment which is available at any moment for transference to entrepreneurs."[38] And again, "Capital is nothing but the lever by which the entrepreneur subjects to his control the concrete goods which he needs, nothing but a means of diverting the factors of production to new uses, or of dictating a new direction to production.[39]

Thus, Schumpeterian capital is not the stock of real assets of a community; it is rather a particular fund of liquid purchasing power. Furthermore, as Schumpeter uses the term, capital is not a factor of production.

> The function of capital consists in procuring for the entrepreneur the means with which to produce. It stands as a third agent necessary to production in an exchange economy *between* the entrepre-

> neur and the world of goods. It constitutes the bridge between them. It does not take part directly in production, it is not itself 'worked up'; on the contrary it performs a task which must be done before technical production can begin.[40]

Role of Credit. Money capital and credit play a special role in a developing Schumpeterian economy:

> The essential function of credit in our sense consists in enabling the entrepreneur to withdraw the producers' goods which he needs from their previous employments, by exercising a demand for them, and thereby to force the economic system into new channels. . . . By credit, entrepreneurs are given access to the social stream of goods before they have acquired the normal claim to it. It temporarily substitutes, as it were, a fiction of this claim for the claim itself. Granting credit in this sense operates as an order on the economic system to accommodate itself to the purposes of the entrepreneur, as an order on the goods which he needs: It means entrusting him with productive forces.[41]

According to Schumpeter, credit is important only if "development" is taking place, and only the entrepreneur requires credit in order to be able to carry on his function. In the absence of "development," the economy is a circular flow economy, in which Say's Law is obeyed.

> For every supply there waits somewhere in the economic system a corresponding demand; for every demand, the corresponding supply. All goods are dealt in at determined prices with only insignificant oscillations, so that every unit of money may be considered as going the same way in every period. A given quantity of purchasing power is available at any moment to purchase the existing quantity of original productive services, in order then to pass into the hands of their owners and then again to be spent in consumption goods.[42]

Hence only when "development" occurs is credit essential.

Credit endows the entrepreneur with claims upon the factors of production before he has created a corresponding value in real goods and services. In the short run, therefore, the granting of credit is inflationary. However, once the fruits of a successful innovation hit the market place, the value added to the social product exceeds the value of the claims created by the amount of the entrepreneurial profit. Thus:

> The equivalence between the money and commodity streams is more than restored, the credit inflation more than eliminated, the

> effect upon prices more than compensated for, so that it may be said that there is no credit inflation at all in this case—rather deflation—but only a non-synchronous appearance of purchasing power and of the commodities corresponding to it, which temporarily produces the semblance of inflation.[43]

With the aid of credit, then, the rate of introduction of innovations is independent of the accumulation of [*ex ante*] savings. Entrepreneurial investment is financed, at least temporarily, out of forced savings.

To summarize, the rate of an economy's "development" is a function of the change in the society's fund of applied technical knowledge. The rate of improvements in the techniques of production depends upon the level of entrepreneurial activity, which is governed by the rate of emergence of new entrepreneurs and the creation of credit.

Grouping of Entrepreneurial Activities. "The new combinations are not, as one would expect, according to general principles of probability, evenly distributed through time . . . but appear, if at all, discontinuously in groups or swarms."[44] The reason for this lies in the fact that the "appearance of one or a few entrepreneurs facilitates the appearance of others, and these the appearance of more, in ever increasing numbers."[45]

First of all:

> Only a few people have these qualities of leadership and only a few in . . . a situation . . . which is not itself already a boom can succeed in this direction. However, if one or a few have advanced with success many of the difficulties disappear. Others can follow these pioneers. . . . Their success again makes it easier . . . for more people to follow suit, until finally the innovation becomes familiar and the acceptance of it a matter of free choice.[46]

Second: since entrepreneurial qualities are distributed according to a normal curve, "the number of individuals who satisfy progressively diminishing standards in this respect continually increase. Hence . . . with the progressive lightening of the task continually more people can and will become entrepreneurs."[47]

Third:

> Reality also disclosed that every normal boom starts in one or a few branches of industry . . . and that it derives its character from the innovations in the industry where it begins. But the pioneers

> remove the obstacles for the others not only in the branch of production in which they first appear, but . . . in other branches too.[48]

Theory of Economic Cycles. The swarm-like appearance of entrepreneurs accounts for the cyclical nature of economic progress. For the clustering of innovations creates a discontinuous disturbance in the economy, which alone suffices to explain the features of a boom.[49] In addition, the bunching of innovations also requires a special process of adaptation of the economy in the form of periodic depressions, "which may therefore be defined from our standpoint as the economic system's struggling towards a new equilibrium position, its adaptation to the data as altered by the disturbance of the boom."[50]

The upper turning point arises because the credit-financed innovations bid up the production factor prices, while the product prices fall when the goods resulting from the innovations suddenly hit the market place.[51] In addition, as the entrepreneurs repay their loans, a credit deflation ensues. No new demand for finance arises at this stage, since, in the meantime, the relationships between product prices and factor prices have made further innovations unprofitable. Losses occur, and the depression persists until the cost price equilibrium stabilizes.[52] Then, a new swarm of innovations appears, and the cyclical process starts all over again. Accordingly, business fluctuations are a permanent feature of the dynamic time path of a capitalistic economy.

The Trend of Growth. Secularly, the progress of a capitalist system is characterized by cyclically induced rising levels of national income and of output per head. Furthermore, the long-run increase in average real income is accompanied by a redistribution of real output in favor of the lower income groups. For, productivity-raising innovations occur primarily in the manufacture of mass-produced commodities, upon which a larger share of a typical worker's budget is spent. Thus, "the capitalist process, not by coincidence but by virtue of its mechanism, progressively raises the standard of life for the masses."[53]

Is there any limit to the increase in the rate of output per head? That is, in the absence of population growth, will a capitalist economy eventually tend to approach a stationary state? Schumpeter said no: since the expansion of output is geared to the rate of innovation [see equation (6.7)], a ceiling upon per capita income would imply that technological progress is subject to historically diminishing returns.

There is no reason to believe that this is the case, however. On the contrary,

> Technological possibilities are an uncharted sea. . . . From the fact that some of them have been exploited before others, it cannot be inferred that the former were more productive than the latter. And those that are still in the lap of the gods may be more or less productive than any that have thus far come within our range of observation. . . . There is no reason to expect slackening of the rate of output through exhaustion of technological possibilities.[54]

PREDICTIONS ON DECLINE OF CAPITALISM

While Schumpeter could see no valid economic reason for the breakdown of capitalism, nevertheless, like Marx before him, he predicted that the capitalist form of society would eventually be superseded by socialism.[55]

First of all, the evolution of capitalism leads to the obsolescence of the entrepreneurial function.[56] By his very success, the entrepreneur creates a socio-economic environment that is adapted to economic change, which it accepts as a matter of course. Innovation therefore becomes easier; the way is paved to make technological progress a routine process. Teams of trained specialists assume the entrepreneurial function. Individual entrepreneurial leadership is replaced by a bureaucracy of highly trained salaried managers. The economic decline of the entrepreneur undermines his social position and, with him, that of the entire *bourgeoisie,* which is dependent upon successful past or present entrepreneurship for the bulk of its income, status, and function.

Second, technological progress uncovers possibilities for economies of scale in production and distribution,[57] with concentration of industry and "big business" the inevitable result. But these forms of market structure tend to undermine the capitalist institutions of private property and freedom of contract. Big corporations substitute salaried executives and managers for entrepreneurs, and stockholders for owners; neither of these corporate groups adequately represents the property interest and spirit. Similarly, the meaning of freedom of contract is subverted by bargaining between business management and union management, rather than by direct agreement between owners and workers. The capitalist process thus tends to undermine the institutional framework of capitalist society.

Capitalism also gives rise to attitudes inimical to its own long-run interests. Thus capitalist rationality and liberalism undermined the institution of monarchy. But according to Schumpeter, the *bourgeoisie* is politically helpless and therefore requires protection by some other agency within the society.[58] Historically, the kings offered the *bourgeoisie* such political support. Hence, "in breaking down the pre-capitalist framework of society, capitalism broke not only barriers that impeded its progress but also flying buttresses that prevented its collapse."[59]

Similarly, capitalist rationalism leads to a disintegration of family life, encouraging the application of "utilitarian calculus" to the problem of optimal family size.[60] The advantages of a larger family are weighed against the disadvantages of smaller per capita real income and freedom, mobility, and leisure. The resulting decline in family size and the weakening of the values of family life diminish the drive to accumulate, which is so fundamental to capitalist ethics.

Finally, capitalism breeds a class of intellectuals, who are endowed with leisure, freedom of speech, and attitudes of rational scientific inquiry.[61] They are trained to criticize. In the social sphere, the intellectuals mobilize, mould, and articulate the feelings of hostility against the existing social order. Weakened by the emasculation of the *bourgeoisie,* by the undermining of the institutions of private property and freedom of contract, by the removal of the protective political barriers, and by the decline of the driving force provided by the family motive, capitalism is particularly vulnerable. Under the impact of constant hostile criticism, the capitalist framework is gradually transformed into a socialist one. Thus, "there is inherent in the capitalist system a tendency towards self-destruction—those factors make not only for the destruction of the capitalist but for the emergence of a socialist civilization."[62]

SUMMARY

Given the rate of population growth, the dynamic evolution of a capitalist economy is determined by its rate of innovation. This rate is a function of entrepreneurial activity, which depends, in turn, upon the distribution of entrepreneurial talent in the population and upon the willingness of credit institutions to finance risky undertakings. Capitalistic institutions, motivations, and rationality are the socio-cultural framework most conducive to the plentiful manifestation of entrepreneurial activity. Since innovations appear in discontinuous swarms, the economic development of a capitalist economy is inherently cyclical in nature. Secularly, continued technological progress will result in an unbounded increase in total and per capita output, since historically there are no diminishing returns to technological progress. As long as technological progress takes place, the rate of profits will be positive. Hence there can be no drying up of sources of investible funds nor any vanishing of investment opportunities. There is therefore no *a priori* ceiling to the level of per capita income in a capitalist society. Nonetheless, the economic success of capitalism will eventually lead to its decay. For the very process of capitalist development weakens the institutions and values basic to its own survival.

What implications does Schumpeter's analysis have for underdeveloped areas? His theory suggests the operation of yet another "vicious circle" in underdeveloped regions. In the last analysis, the incidence and characteristics of entrepreneurial activity are determined by the socio-cultural environment of the economy. But the rate of change of the institutional and socio-cultural environment is itself a function of the rate of innovation. Therefore in a society in which the socio-cultural milieu is not conducive to entrepreneurship, the traditional patterns and values will persist. The stagnation of the socio-cultural framework will in turn react adversely upon the entrepreneurial potential. Thus the vicious circle of low levels of entrepreneurial activity, of slow rates of growth of output, and of stagnant social institutions and values tends to be self-perpetuating.

SEVEN

A NEO-KEYNESIAN MODEL OF A GROWING ECONOMY

OUR PURPOSE in this chapter is to explore with the aid of a single model several contemporary theories of growth and development. This model will combine certain features of classical Marxian and Schumpeterian dynamics with more recent contributions to the analysis of economic growth.[1] Thus, while the spirit of this model is classical in nature, some of the concepts and tools are more modern. We hope that the consequences of certain classical and neo-classical assumptions will become clearer as a result of the analysis. Furthermore, to the extent that the postulates are applicable to real situations, the conclusions implied by the model will possess a certain degree of general validity.

NATURE OF THE MODEL ECONOMY

The economy we postulate consists of a two-class society, workers and capitalist-entrepreneurs.[2] The workers simply supply labor and consume; the capitalist-entrepreneurs manage business enterprises, own property, supply capital to their firms, lend and borrow from one another, and also consume. There are, therefore, two general types of income, namely, wages and profits, where the term "profits" is taken to include also interest and rent. All wage income as well as a part of profit income is consumed; the remaining portion of profit is saved and invested.

For simplicity, we also assume that there are two factors of production: labor and capital. Land and natural resources are considered to constitute a portion of the economy's capital stock.[3] Furthermore, we confine our remarks to an economy that is, on the average, in a state of full employment of all factors.

The time period chosen for the analysis is sufficiently long to permit investment to affect the economy's productive capacity during the same period in which the investment is made.[4] Whereas population size varies during the unit-period, the time interval is so selected that current changes in population will not affect the size of the labor force in the current period, but will be reflected entirely in the period that follows.*

Finally, we must say something about the structure of our specific model. As pointed out in the general framework presented in Chapter Two, there are six basic equations [(2.1), (2.3)–(2.7)] governing the time path of the economy, which relate the variables Y, K, L, N, S, and U. We shall take the last of these variables to be exogenous, and the next to the last to be determined (with no implications about causality) by an implicit relationship among S, U, and t. Since we assume that N is amalgamated (in some manner or other) with K, we are left with three relationships to discuss in the remainder of this chapter. We shall first examine the pattern of growth of the labor force in the economy, then analyze the savings-investment equilibrium. Later, we shall use the production function of the economy to study the interactions among accumulation, labor growth, and per capita output. At the end of this chapter, we shall analyze the economy's long-run dynamic behavior as it approaches equilibrium with and without technological progress, and with and without constant returns to scale.

POPULATION GROWTH AND THE LABOR FORCE

The rate of increase of the labor force, which we require as one of the input functions to our model, obviously depends upon the rate of population growth. For convenience, we shall assume that the entire change in the labor force in a given period is due to the change of population in the preceding period, and that the same percentage of the total population is employed at the beginning of each period. Since we also assume full employment at all times, we may equate the percentage increase in the labor force to the percentage growth of population during the $(t-1)$st period. In order that we may understand the character of variation in the supply of labor, then, we must investigate the determinants of population growth.

* This implies either that population is constant or increasing, or that any decline in population occurs among age groups not included in the labor force.

We shall adopt classical postulates concerning population expansion. That is, we assume that at a given level of income and within a given socio-cultural context the rate of population growth varies with the distribution of income between classes.[5] Of course, the nature and extent of the dependence of population growth upon the distribution of income varies with the level of income. Furthermore, the response of population to changes in relative shares is also heavily conditioned by the customs, outlook, religion, and institutions of the country in question.

We may reasonably assume that the dependence of population growth upon the distribution of income is most pronounced at low levels of per capita income. Even when the over-all average standard of living is low, the per capita income of profit receivers is so high that mortality rates within the entrepreneurial class are not particularly sensitive to changes in income. In contrast, at low levels of income the rate of growth of the working class must be quite heavily income-dependent. A higher wage rate stimulates the growth of the laboring population by reducing mortality rates through the better nutrition, health, and sanitation standards that accompany improved wages. Birth rates also rise, since a larger percentage of live births stems from the better health conditions of women of child-bearing age. As a result, at low per capita incomes a redistribution of income in favor of wage earners generally augments the population growth rate, whereas an increase in the share of profit receivers generally reduces the pace of population expansion.

We assume that the functional relationship between the rate of population growth and the wage rate has the general character of the curve *OP* in Figure 7.1. The percentage change in population per period p_t is portrayed along the vertical axis; the horizontal axis represents w_t, the excess of the real wage rate over the subsistence wage level. Whenever the wage rate rises slightly above subsistence, there is a strong impetus to population growth. The stimulus is due to the rapid drop in

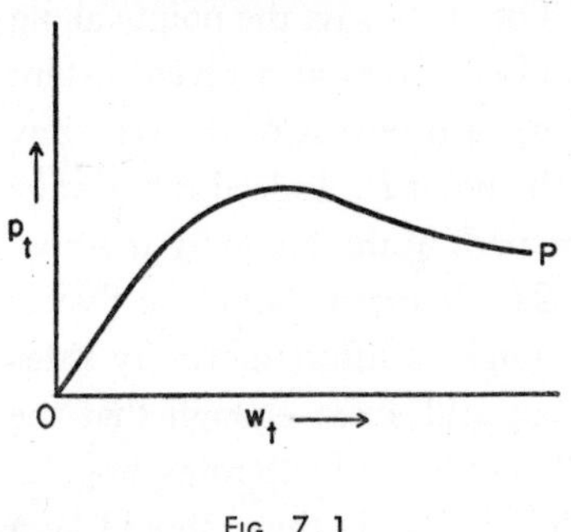

FIG. 7.1

both infant and adult mortality that follows the increase in wages. Since the birth rate is substantially unaffected, the phase of population explosion is launched. If the wage rate continues to rise, death rates will decline further, but birth rates will begin to drop under the impact of urbanization, industrialization, and the higher status of women. Therefore, population will continue to expand as the wage rate moves up, but at a decreasing rate.

Since the reduction in mortality rates is limited by medical technology, whereas the sociological impact of improved living standards upon birth rates reaches a larger and larger segment of the population, the rate of population growth will sooner or later reach some maximum value $p_{\max}$. However, if there is a large enough segment of the population for which a rise in wage rates leads to a decrease in the desired family size, the rate of population growth will later fall below $p_{\max}$. Eventually, as wage rates continue to rise, the rate of population growth will tend to level off at some value $\bar{p}$, since there must be some minimum desired family size for the population as a whole. With customs, religious values, and other socio-cultural influences playing a predominant role in determining individual attitudes toward the desired rate of reproduction, the magnitude of $\bar{p}$ and the minimum wage level associated with it will, of course, vary from society to society and from culture to culture. We assume that, in general, $\bar{p} > 0$.

Note that the curve OP is not drawn on *caeteris paribus* assumptions. On the contrary, simultaneously with a rise in wage rates, certain changes in human attitudes and motivations and in the institutional and cultural climate are assumed to take place. Because of these changes, and regardless of their detailed nature in a particular case, OP has a dynamic rather than a static character. That is to say, the points along the curve do not exist as simultaneous alternatives at a given instant of time; rather, they represent the historical progress of the economy in its movement from the origin toward the point P. Indeed if the wage rate does not increase monotonically, the path of the economy is somewhat more complicated (see Figure 7.2). If there should be fluctuations in wage rates over times long enough to affect mortality rates through health and sanitation factors, but still short enough that the sociological effects (urbanization, etc,) do not lower birth rates, population may follow a path like $OABACDCEFEP$. If there should be a long-term fluctuation instead, the path may look more like $OABA'B'P$ in Figure 7.3. And, depending on the relative influence of wages on mortality and on birth rates, the point B' may lie above or below the

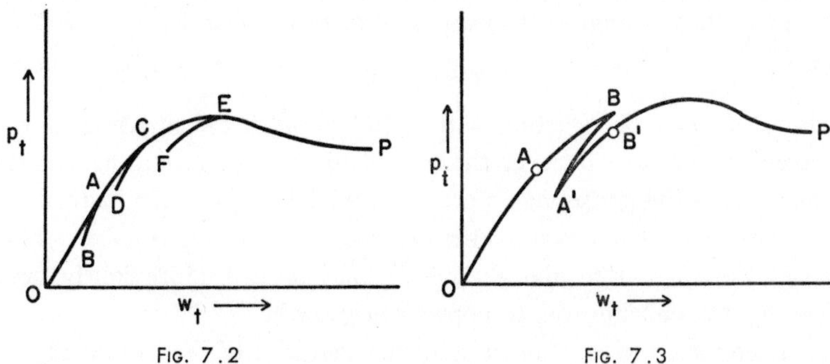

FIG. 7.2

FIG. 7.3

point B. The detailed shape of these curves also depends on the long-term rate at which wages are changing through time; in fact, the location of B' may be significantly affected by the rate of rise of w between A' and B'. In short, the path described by the economy in its movement from O to P is not reversible. Nevertheless, the path of the economy can be represented qualitatively to a good approximation by the simple curve OP of Figure 7.1.

At the start of each period, the labor force consists of the labor employed in the previous period plus some fraction of the increment to population during a previous period. A certain amount of current capital accumulation will therefore be required to bring up the capital–labor ratio to what it was at the end of the previous period. Since the percentage change in the capital–labor ratio (q_t) is precisely $k_t - l_t$ (where k_t is the percentage change in capital and l_t is the percentage change in the labor force) and since $l_t = p_{t-1}$ is independent of events in the current period (by hypothesis), the graph of q_t as a function of k_t is simply the straight line shown in Figure 7.4.

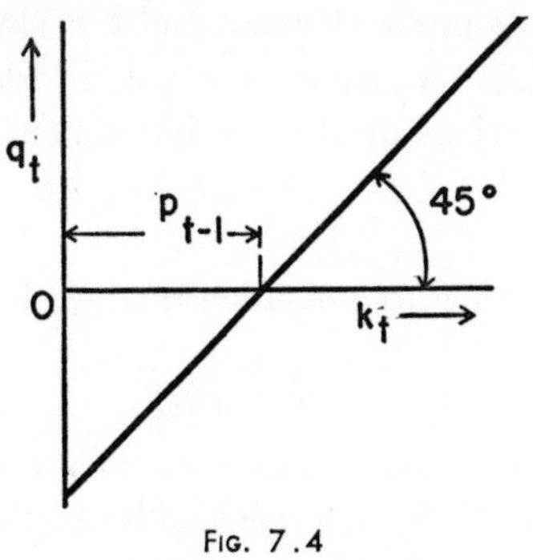

FIG. 7.4

We assume that the character of innovations is not sufficiently labor-displacing to enable capital accumulation to take place without increasing the demand for labor somewhat. This implies that in the long run changes in the real wage rate are an increasing function of the percentage change of the capital–labor ratio. That is,

$$dw_t/dt = f(q_t)\,, \tag{7.1}$$

where $\partial f/\partial q_t > 0$. Starting with a full-employment situation in the preceding period, whenever the percentage rate of capital accumulation exceeds the percentage increase of the labor force, the increase in the demand for labor exceeds the increase in the supply of labor. This raises the wage rate above the rate that prevailed previously, and thereby gives an impetus to population growth.

Therefore, the clue to the long-run behavior of population in our model must be sought in the behavior of the capital–labor ratio. Since this, in turn, depends partially upon the nature of the equilibrium between savings and investment, and partially upon the technical character of production, it is necessary to investigate both of these functions before one can completely understand the growth of the labor force.

THE SAVINGS-INVESTMENT FUNCTION

Our savings assumption is Marxian in nature.[6] We postulate that the capitalist-entrepreneurs save a constant proportion of their earnings independent of time, and that wage receipts are devoted solely to consumer expenditures; i.e.,

$$S = \alpha P\,, \tag{7.2}$$

where S stands for savings, P represents profit incomes, and α is the average propensity to save out of profits. A necessary condition for equilibrium growth is, of course, that savings must equal investment:

$$S = I\,. \tag{7.3}$$

Hence, the equilibrium percentage of capital accumulation is given by

$$k = \alpha P/K = \alpha r\,, \tag{7.4}$$

where r is the average rate of return on investment. This equation states that the equilibrium percentage rate of capital expansion is strictly proportional to the average rate of profit.[7] In Figure 7.5 the hori-

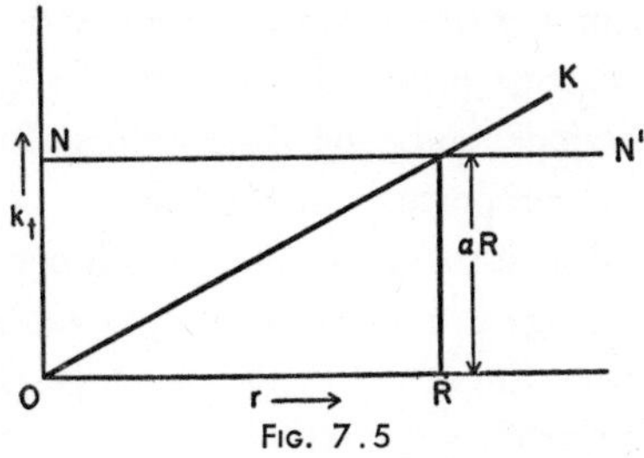

Fig. 7.5

zontal axis represents the rate of profit r, the vertical coordinate measures the percentage growth rate of capital k. The line OK, whose slope is α, therefore depicts the various percentage rates of accumulation at which savers will be satisfied to continue saving at the same rate. In R. F. Harrod's terminology,[8] then, the line OK portrays the locus of warranted rates of growth of capital* as a function of the rate of profit. If and only if the point defined by the actual rate of accumulation and the rate of profit lies on this line, is the point a potential equilibrium position.

Unlike Harrod's model, however, our model does not generate a unique warranted rate of growth of capital,† unless the rate of profit is given. To any given rate of profit corresponds a single equilibrium rate of accumulation G_w. Whenever there is a change in the rate of profit, one would expect the share of profits P/Y to be altered; simultaneously, a new value for the desired capital–output ratio K/Y will emerge because the entrepreneurs can increase profits by substituting capital for labor or vice versa. The share of profits, of course, governs the propensity to save out of a given level of income, and the target capital–output ratio determines the propensity to invest by influencing the size of the desired capital stock at any level of output. Thus, variations in the warranted rate of accumulation with the rate of profit will be accompanied by simultaneous adjustments in both the savings and the investment propensities of the community.[9] Symbolically, one can arrive at the same conclusion by noting that

$$G_w = \alpha r = \alpha \frac{P}{K} = \alpha \frac{P/Y}{K/Y}. \tag{7.5}$$

Let us now look at the relative importance of the share of profits

---

* Harrod defines the warranted rate of growth as that rate of advance which, if carried out, will leave entrepreneurs prepared to carry on a similar advance. (See *Dynamic Economics*, p. 82.)

† Harrod does not provide for capital deepening in response to a fall in the rate of interest (*ibid*, p. 86). However, note that in our model the rate of profit (and not the rate of interest) appears as a determinant of G_w.

and the capital–output ratio in determining the warranted rate of the economy's growth. The percentage change in the share of profits is precisely the percentage change in savings, since, by assumption, the capitalist-entrepreneurs save a constant proportion of this (profit) income. On the other hand, since annual investment is only a small percentage of the capital stock, a small change in the capital–output ratio requires a large change in investment. Empirical evidence suggests that yearly movements in the share of profit are of the same order of magnitude as those in the capital–output ratio. We shall assume that this state of affairs exists throughout the approach to long-run equilibrium. Hence, the warranted rate of growth is much more sensitive to movements in the capital–output ratio than it is to changes in the share of profits. Evidently, it is the desired rate of investment rather than the desired rate of savings which is the primary determinant of actual investment and therefore of changes in the warranted rate of growth.

In view of the above discussion, it is reasonable in our model to postulate that changes in the desired capital–output ratio are the *sole* determinant of movements in the warranted rate of accumulation.* If the rate of output increase exceeds the rate of capital increase, accumulation will be stepped up. Conversely, if the expansion of capital were to outrun the increase in production, the capital–output ratio will decline and accumulation will be curtailed. Therefore, the only unconstrained rate of capital accumulation that will tend to maintain itself in the long run (i.e., the only possible long-run point of equilibrium) prevails when capital and output are expanding hand in hand and when the capital–output ratio is constant.

This rate corresponds to G_n, Harrod's natural rate of growth of capital.† In the context of an expanding economy the natural rate may be defined as the rate of growth of capital that keeps the capital–output ratio constant under given rates of technical progress and population growth. The economy will be in long-run equilibrium only if savers and investors are content to accumulate capital at the percentage rate

* This argument is similar in spirit to that of Kaldor, "Model," pp. 611–12. For a different approach, which depends, however, on marginal productivity theory and upon the shape of the production function, see footnote on p. 119.

† Harrod, in *Dynamic Economics,* p. 87, defines the natural rate of growth as the rate of advance which the increase of population and technological improvements allow.

indicated by G_n. In other words, a necessary condition for long-run equilibrium in our model is that the warranted rate of growth of capital be equal to the natural rate:[10]

$$G_w = G_n. \tag{7.6}$$

Graphically, if the natural rate of growth of capital is portrayed by a line like NN' in Figure 7.5, the long-run equilibrium position of accumulation is given by ON, and the long-run equilibrium value of profit is given by OR.

A necessary condition for the stability of this equilibrium position in a free-enterprise economy is that rising capital–output ratios be associated with rates of accumulation larger than G_n, and conversely, that falling capital–output ratios be accompanied by rates of increase on capital smaller than G_n. Then, if the actual rate of accumulation is less than ON, investment will be accelerated; and if the actual rate of investment is greater than ON, investment will slow down. Whether or not the capital–output ratio behaves in this manner depends upon the technical character of production.

THE PRODUCTION FUNCTION

For the sake of simplicity, we assume that the productive relationships in the community may be approximated by a Cobb-Douglas production function.* Then, in the absence of technological progress, we may write that

$$Y = K^{\beta} L^{\gamma}, \tag{7.7}$$

where β is the (constant) elasticity of output with respect to capital [i.e., $\beta = (\partial Y/\partial K)/(Y/K)$], and γ is the similarly defined (constant) elasticity of output with respect to labor.† With constant returns to

* The same production function appears in Swan, "Economic Growth and Capital Accumulation." Solow, in "A Contribution to the Theory of Economic Growth," uses a Cobb-Douglas function with constant returns to scale. A generalized production function with a constant elasticity of substitution between capital and labor, which is not necessarily either zero or unity, is given in an unpublished paper by K. J. Arrow, H. B. Chenery, Robert Solow, and B. Minhas, "Substitution between Capital and Labor."

† If we assume that each factor is rewarded in proportion to its marginal product, β and γ are also the relative shares of capital and labor, respectively.

scale, $\beta + \gamma = 1$. If there are economies of scale, $\beta + \gamma > 1$, and if production is subject to diminishing returns, $\beta + \gamma < 1$. We assume that, under any circumstances, β and γ are each positive but less than unity; this hypothesis is consistent with empirical data. Let us define

(7.8) $$\delta = 1 - \beta - \gamma .$$

Then, $\delta = 0$ if returns to scale are constant, $\delta < 0$ if there are increasing returns, and $\delta > 0$ for the case of diminishing returns. With this definition, output per worker Y/L becomes

(7.9) $$\frac{Y}{L} = \left(\frac{K}{L}\right)^{\beta} L^{-\delta} .$$

The rate of change of output per man is then given by

(7.10)
$$\frac{d}{dt}\left(\frac{Y}{L}\right) = -\delta L^{-\delta-1}\left(\frac{K}{L}\right)^{\beta}\frac{dL}{dt} + \beta L^{-\delta}\left(\frac{K}{L}\right)^{\beta-1}\frac{d}{dt}\left(\frac{K}{L}\right) .$$

If we divide both sides of (7.10) by (7.9), the percentage rate of growth of output per man z becomes

(7.11) $$z = -\delta l + \beta q ,$$

where q is the percentage rate of growth of the capital–labor ratio, and l is the relative rate of growth of labor.

Constant Returns to Scale. The relative rate of change of output per worker is portrayed as a function of the percentage rate of change of the capital–labor ratio in Figure 7.6. For the case of constant returns to scale ($\delta = 0$), the graph of (7.11) is a straight line Y_1Y_1' through the origin with a slope of β. If the capital–labor ratio remains constant with time, output per man does not change. As the capital–labor ratio increases, output per worker rises β times as much. But since $\beta < 1$, the slope of Y_1Y_1' must be smaller than unity. This implies that throughout the entire positive range the rate of change of output per man is smaller than the rate of change of capital per man, so that the capital–output ratio is rising. We saw earlier, however, that the only possible long-run equilibrium position for capital accumulation is one at which the capital–output ratio is constant.* With a rising capital–

* See the argument in the previous section, p. 116.

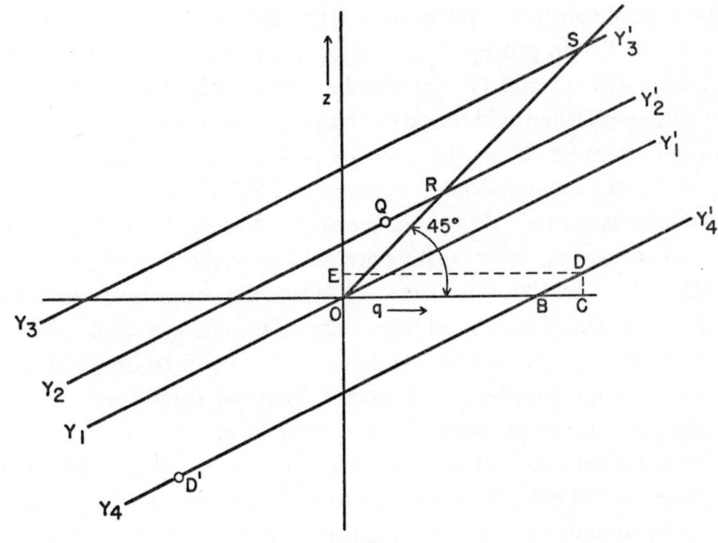

FIG. 7.6

output ratio the average productivity of capital is falling,* and hence the rate of capital accumulation slows down. The resultant decrease in the rate of change of the capital–labor ratio is reflected in a fall in the rate of increase of wages and consequently in the rate of growth of the labor force. Hence the only long-run equilibrium solution for the case of constant returns to scale (in the absence of technological change) is one in which output per worker is constant and capital per man unchanged.

Graphically, this situation exists at the origin O. That this is a potential equilibrium state may also be seen mathematically. If the capital–output ratio is to remain unchanged, the percentage rate of increase of output per worker must equal the percentage rate of increase of capital per worker. That is

$$z = q \tag{7.12}$$

But from (7.11) we have

$$z = \beta q \tag{7.13}$$

* If the rate of profit equals the marginal product of capital, we get from (7.7) that $r = \beta(Y/K)$. Under these circumstances, the rate of profit would vary in strict proportion to the average product of capital. Cf. Swan, "Economic Growth," p. 335.

in the case of constant returns ($\delta = 0$). Since some labor is required for any production process, β cannot be equal to unity. Therefore, we can satisfy (7.12) and (7.13) simultaneously only if $z = q = 0$. In long-run equilibrium with constant returns to scale and with no technological progress, then, the average productivity of labor must be constant, and capital and labor must grow hand in hand.

So long as the rate of profit at the origin exceeds the minimum rate of return consistent with positive accumulation, the rate of growth of capital will be greater than zero. If, when the economy attains this point, a sufficiently high level of per capita income has been achieved to guarantee that the rate of population growth will be essentially independent of the distribution of income, long-run equilibrium will obviously imply a rate of population growth $\bar{p} = k$.

On the other hand, along that part of the population curve OP in which the rate of growth is sensitive to wage income, any point can be a position of equilibrium, provided that $k = l$ and the capital–output ratio is constant. Furthermore, along the rising portion of the population curve any such equilibrium will be stable with respect to small displacements. Thus, at a point B along OP in Figure 7.1, if the rate of accumulation is suddenly displaced upward from its equilibrium value $k_B = l_B = p_B$, so that the new rate of accumulation $k'_B > l_B$, the capital–labor ratio increases, and hence the wage rate [see equation (7.2)] goes up. The rise in the capital–labor ratio also increases the average productivity of labor [see equation (7.13)]. But since $\beta < 1$, the rate of increase of productivity will be lower than the rate of rise of the capital–labor ratio. Therefore, the capital–output ratio will rise, and hence accumulation will decline toward k_B.

This process will continue until the rate of capital accumulation equals the rate of increase of the labor force l_B, which by hypothesis is equal to p_{t-1}, and therefore is fixed for the t'th period. However, since the temporary rise in the capital–labor ratio has increased the wage rate above what it would have been otherwise, the population growth rate during the period temporarily expands. The capital–labor ratio soon returns to its previous value (let us assume that the time required for the adjustment is much less than one period), and hence the wage rate and the rate of population growth do likewise (to a first approximation).

At the end of the period, then, there is a larger population and a larger capital stock than there would have been without the temporary increase in capital. The larger population leads to an additional jump in the labor force as we pass from this period into the next. If the disturbance is sufficiently small, the capital–labor ratio at the beginning of the new period will be approximately the same as it was before the disturbance. Similar events during the next period will tend to reduce further whatever discrepancy may remain. As a result of all these interactions, the net effect of the disturbance is to raise K, L, and Y to values higher than would have existed if this perturbation had not occurred. On the other hand, all the growth rates, the capital–output and capital–labor ratios, and the wage rate are approximately unchanged. A similar argument can be made for any other small displacement from equilibrium; therefore, the equilibrium attained at B is stable for small displacements.

The equilibrium of an economy with unchanging technology in which constant returns to scale prevail is therefore described by a situation in which the capital growth rate is equal to some arbitrary labor growth rate. Since this rate of accumulation also keeps the capital–output ratio constant, we have the natural rate of capital growth (G_n) equal to the rate of population growth. That is, a necessary condition for long-run equilibrium is that

$$G_w = G_n = k = p \,. \tag{7.14}$$

As a result, of course, output per worker is also steady. In fact, the long-run equilibrium state of such an economy is Mrs. Robinson's "golden age"[11]—a period in which capital, output, and labor are all growing at the same percentage rate.

Increasing Returns. Let us now investigate the dynamic process in an economy in which production is subject to increasing returns. As explained by Adam Smith,* increasing returns arise because certain production techniques and certain forms of industrial organization that are not practical on a smaller scale become economically feasible as markets expand.[12] Thus, possibilities for internal and external economies can materialize even without advances in knowledge. The tech-

---

* See Chapter Three.

nical changes required to exploit economies of scale, incidentally, are Schumpeterian innovations, regardless of whether or not the fund of scientific knowledge has increased in the process.

The extent to which economies of scale are realized in a given society depends upon the willingness and ability of firms to alter their methods of production.[13] In addition, the degree of increasing returns depends also upon the economy's capacity to modify the organization of industry by such structural changes as the creation of new specialized industries to perform functions previously ancillary to another industry, the introduction of new methods of distribution and new channels of marketing, etc. Hence the time rate at which economies of scale evolve is a function of economic flexibility and of human adaptability to change. The extent of exploitation of economies of scale depends partly upon the nature of the socio-cultural environment. Furthermore, since the exploitation of different technical possibilities generally requires changes in the form of the capital stock, the degree of realization of increasing returns depends also upon the average rate of gross investment.

The case of increasing returns to scale is depicted graphically in Figure 7.6 by the line Y_2Y_2'.[14] It is apparent from (7.11) that since (by hypothesis) the current rate of increase of the labor force is independent of current changes in the capital–labor ratio, Y_2Y_2' must be parallel to Y_1Y_1' and displaced vertically upward from it by an amount equal to $-\delta l$. The upward shift of Y_2Y_2' relative to Y_1Y_1' thus depends both upon the growth rate of the labor force (l) and upon the degree of increasing returns (δ).

A necessary condition for long-run equilibrium, as we have seen, is that the capital–output ratio be constant. At point R in Figure 7.6 (defined by the intersection of Y_2Y_2' with the line $z = q$) the percentage rate of growth of capital per worker equals the percentage rate of increase of output per man. At this point, the capital–output ratio is constant, and the economy can be in long-run equilibrium. However, as the economy moves from point Q, for example, toward point R, the resultant increase in the capital–labor ratio leads to an increase in wages, and therefore to a corresponding movement in the population growth rate. In the following period, this new rate of population growth is reflected in a change in l and therefore in a shift in Y_2Y_2'.

This process will continue until the wage rate is sufficiently large to make the rate of increase of population (and therefore of the labor force) independent of wages. The economy is stable in the case of increasing returns only if $l = \bar{p}$ (point S on Y_3Y_3'). Even if the economy is at a point such as R, for which the capital–output ratio is constant, but $l \neq \bar{p}$, there will not be long-run equilibrium, since the rising capital–labor ratio will force wages up and therefore change the growth rate of the labor force.

The rate of capital accumulation which corresponds to S is, of course, the natural rate of capital growth G_n ; we may find this rate mathematically by setting

$$z = q = m \,, \tag{7.15}$$

which is a constant. Substituting into (7.11) and remembering that $l = \bar{p}$ and $\delta < 0$, we have

$$m = -\delta\bar{p} + \beta m \,; \tag{7.16}$$

or

$$m = -\delta\bar{p}/(1-\beta) \,, \tag{7.17}$$

which is a positive quantity. The natural rate of capital growth is given in this case by

$$k = q + l = m + \bar{p} = \frac{\bar{p}(1-\beta-\delta)}{1-\beta} = \bar{p}\,\frac{\gamma}{1-\beta} \,. \tag{7.18}$$

It appears, therefore, that the equilibrium rate of capital growth in the long run is determined solely by the equilibrium rate of population growth $\bar{p}$ and by technical considerations $\delta/(1 - \beta)$, and is independent of the community's propensity to save.[15] The propensity to save affects only the equilibrium rate of profit, since in equilibrium $G_w = G_n$, and

$$r = \frac{G_n}{\alpha} = \bar{p}\frac{\gamma}{\alpha(1-\beta)} \,. \tag{7.19}$$

Equilibrium for the case of increasing returns to scale is therefore characterized by a situation in which the average product of labor and hence per capita income are increasing at a constant percentage rate.

Population is expanding at an unconstrained rate. Capital accumulation proceeds at a rate that is sufficient to equip the growing labor force with an increasing amount of capital. The economy is in what may be termed a "platinum age."

Let us investigate the stability of this equilibrium. If the economy should suddenly be displaced to a point Q' along Y_3Y_3' to the left of S, the output per worker will increase with time faster than the capital–labor ratio. Therefore at this point the capital–output ratio will decrease with time. There will be a strong tendency for additional accumulation, to take advantage of the fact that the average productivity of capital rises with time. The resultant increase in capital formation moves the capital–labor ratio back up toward its previous value. Since an efficient economy will remain on its production function Y_3Y_3', it will tend to return toward S. During the return process, however, the capital–labor ratio will fall, since the percentage change in the capital–labor ratio is less than the percentage change in the average productivity of labor. On the other hand, although the economy will still return to S from a point such as Q'' (above S), the return will take place under conditions such that the percentage change in the capital–labor ratio exceeds the change in productivity. As a result, the capital–labor ratio falls. In other words, at S the long-run equilibrium is stable,* and the capital–output ratio is a minimum (for a given economy).

Diminishing Returns. The equilibrium state of an economy in which diminishing returns to scale prevail is different in character. This situation might arise, for example, from the existence of a third factor of production, such as land,[16] which is fixed in quantity and quality. Since we assume that there is full employment of all factors of production, the same amount of the third factor will be used under any conditions, and therefore the factor will not appear directly in the differentiated form [equation (7.11)] of the per-worker production func-

* Harrod argued that this situation is unstable. See his *Dynamic Economics,* pp. 87–100. However, Solow, "Economic Growth," and Swan, "Economic Growth," show that the Harrodian instability is removed when substitution in production can take place. Tobin in "Dynamic Aggregative Model" and Kaldor in "Model" demonstrate that the instability disappears when savings ratios are allowed to vary with portfolio structure and entrepreneurial incomes. In our system, both savings ratios (*ex post*) and capital requirements vary to reach equilibrium.

tion. Rather, its effects are included by making $\beta + \gamma < 1$, i.e., by postulating diminishing returns. Graphically, the case of decreasing returns to scale corresponds to the line Y_4Y_4' in Figure 7.6, a line with a slope of β and a positive horizontal intercept $OB = -\delta l$, since δ is greater than zero this time.

We may investigate the dynamic behavior of such an economy by assuming that we start from a situation in which the population is growing at its unconstrained rate $\bar{p}$. Then, if the pace of capital accumulation generates a rate of increase in the capital–labor ratio equal to OC in Figure 7.6, OB of the increase per period is absorbed in offsetting the impact of diminishing returns, and only BC contributes to a rise in per capita output of the economy. Since CD, the rate of change of per capita output, is necessarily smaller than OC, the capital–output ratio is rising, the average productivity of capital is falling, and hence the rate of accumulation in the next period will tend to be reduced. As long as the reduced accumulation still suffices to induce the same rate of population growth $\bar{p}$, the slowing down of the investment rate lowers the rate of increase of output per head only by decreasing the rate of expansion of the capital–labor ratio (i.e., by moving point D to the left). Point D will continue to move to the left along Y_4Y_4' until the capital–labor ratio begins to decline fast enough to bring the economy into a state in which the population growth rate becomes sensitive to the wage rate.

During this process, the economy may reach a point D' such that the rate of decline of output per worker exactly matches the rate of decrease of the capital–labor ratio, leaving the capital–output ratio constant. Such a position, however, is not a true position of equilibrium, since the wage rate is falling at this point. Sooner or later, the wage rate must sink to a value low enough to decrease the rate of population growth. At this time, regardless of whether or not the economy ever reaches D', the change in the population growth rate results in an upward shift of Y_4Y_4', which tends to counteract the effect of the reduction in the capital–labor ratio upon output. Despite this, however, in the new position, output per head is still rising at a slower rate than capital per head. The average productivity of capital therefore continues to fall. Accumulation proceeds at yet a slower pace and so does population expansion. Line Y_4Y_4' continues to shift upward. Equilibrium in this economy is finally reached only when Y_4Y_4' passes through the origin, and when population, capital, and output have all ceased growing. The capital–output ratio at this point is constant, and the economy has reached the stationary state, which is the classical state of equilibrium.

Mathematically, for the case of diminishing returns, the equilibrium value of the rate of growth of the capital–labor ratio is derived as before, to yield an expression that is analogous to (7.17), i.e.,

$$m = -\delta l/(1-\beta)\,. \tag{7.20}$$

However, since δ is now positive, the only possible equilibrium position with constant labor growth would be the one in which output per head and the average productivity of capital were both continually falling. Inasmuch as these circumstances would lead to a decline in population, and therefore in the labor force itself, l must be zero. Hence, as stated above, the only long-run equilibrium position with diminishing returns and without technical progress is precisely the classical stationary state.

To summarize, we have seen that the eventual development of an economy depends upon the technical nature of its production. An economy in which production is characterized by increasing returns to scale tends toward a stable equilibrium state in which output per head is rising and population is growing at its unconstrained rate. An economy with constant returns to scale tends toward a stable long-run equilibrium in which output per head is constant and population expands at any rate consistent with the population curve. Finally, an economy in which diminishing returns prevail tends toward a situation in which output per head is fixed and population size is stable.

In the absence of technological progress, one might expect an economy to pass through three stages. (1) In the first stage the supplies of all factors are variable, since existing stocks of the non-reproducible resources have not all been absorbed in production. Under these circumstances, increasing returns would prevail, provided that the economic structure is sufficiently flexible to permit the techniques of production and the organization of industry to be altered as necessary to take advantage of internal and external economies. (2) As enough resources become fixed in supply, the advantages of increasing returns exactly counterbalance the increasing costs due to the existence of the fixed factors. At this stage, constant returns prevail. (3) Eventually, however, as population continues to expand, the supplies of more and more resources become fixed. Economies of scale, with constant techniques, become insufficient to offset the impact of the fixed factors. Diminishing returns set in, and the economy proceeds toward the stationary state.

TECHNICAL PROGRESS

If we now introduce continuing technological progress into our economy, we can transform a situation that is basically one of diminishing returns into one that appears to have the characteristics of constant or even increasing returns. Consider, for example, two equally durable machines A and B, which require the same number of man-hours and no capital for their construction.* If by using B an entrepreneur can produce more output with less labor than he can by using A, a switch from A to B will raise output per worker and increase the rate of profit on capital.† Some substitutions of capital equipment increase output per unit of capital and reduce the labor–capital ratio; others have their impact primarily through one or the other of these factors. In any case, the criterion for their implementation will be the amount of profit that can be earned from the substitution. Technological progress thus provides opportunities for a hierarchy of substitutions of capital equipment in order of profitability. It also permits improvements in the organization of production to take place. These innovations increase output per man without the substitution of one piece of capital equipment for another, and therefore require little or no investment for their implementation.

The rate of technological progress per unit of time depends largely

---

* These assumptions are made to keep the costs of the two machines identical, regardless of changes in factor costs. Cf. Little, "Classical Growth," p. 163.

† Total profits may be written as $P = Y - wL$, where w is the wage rate. The rate of profit on capital then becomes $P/K = Y/K - w(L/K)$. If we assume that the wage rates are unchanged, we find that changes in the rate of profit depend upon

$$\frac{d}{dt}\left(\frac{P}{K}\right) = \frac{d}{dt}\left(\frac{Y}{K}\right) - w\frac{d}{dt}\left(\frac{L}{K}\right).$$

upon factors similar to those that determine the degree of realization of economies of scale in the absence of advances in human knowledge. As before, the crucial determinant of what Kaldor calls the "technical dynamism"[17] of a society is the willingness of the system to adopt new techniques. This, in turn, depends upon the availability of entrepreneurial talent and upon the receptiveness of the community's economic, social, and institutional fabric to change. Some societies cling to traditional ways of doing things and are rather slow in exploiting and absorbing new techniques. Others have developed a system whose entire economic structure is oriented toward the smooth and rapid diffusion of innovations. In particular, the adoption of organizational changes is likely to depend most strongly upon the degree of flexibility of the social and institutional structure, since innovations of this type alter the structure of society directly.

Two other important determinants of a community's technological progress are the amount of technical training and the degree of inventiveness of its members. However, the second factor is not likely to be crucial in explaining inter-country differences in technical progress in a world characterized by international travel, foreign study, and technical aid.

For the sake of mathematical simplicity we shall assume that technological progress is neutral,* in the sense that the marginal rate of substitution of capital for labor (i.e., the ratio of the marginal products) is unaffected by technical change. Furthermore, we postulate that technological progress proceeds at a uniform rate s per unit time. Then we may incorporate technological progress into our production function by writing

$$Y = Ae^{st}K^{\beta}L^{\gamma}. \tag{7.21}$$

Hence, output per worker becomes

$$\frac{Y}{L} = Ae^{st}\left(\frac{K}{L}\right)^{\beta} L^{-\delta}. \tag{7.22}$$

---

* This postulate is made by Solow, "A Contribution," p. 85, and by Swan, "Economic Growth," p. 338. It appears to be empirically valid. Cf. Robert Solow, "Technical Change and the Aggregate Production Function," *Review of Economics and Statistics,* XXXIX, August 1957, pp. 312–30. The consequences of relaxing this assumption are investigated below (p. 132).

That is, technological development raises the average product of labor corresponding to a given capital stock and labor force. Differentiating (7.22) and dividing the result by Y/L, we obtain the following percentage rate of growth of output per head:

$$z = -\delta l + \beta q + s \,. \tag{7.23}$$

Thus technological progress shifts the lines of Figure 7.6 upward by an amount S along the z-axis, compared with the situation in the absence of technical progress. In particular, technical advance permits some increases in output per man to occur during each period, even without variations in capital and labor. There are basically two economic reasons for this. First, as pointed out earlier, certain technical improvements are purely organizational in nature. Second, replacement investment now takes the form of more productive capital equipment. When the labor force is increasing at a rate l, the net accumulation required to maintain the capital–labor ratio at its previous value takes the same form. In general, then, technological improvement leads also to increases in the average product of capital.

Assume now that the pressure exerted by population upon the economy's fixed resources is large enough in relation to the forces establishing economies of scale to impose, in the absence of technological progress, diminishing returns upon the economy (that is, suppose $\delta > 0$). Returns to scale will then depend upon the value of $s - \delta l$. If the economy's rate of technological development s exceeds δl, the economy will behave as though production is subject to increasing returns. If $s = \delta l$, the dynamic motion of the economy will correspond to that of a system with constant returns. Otherwise, technical progress will merely serve to soften the impact of diminishing returns.

The influence of technical progress upon an economy which in its absence would be subject to diminishing returns may also be analyzed graphically. Let YY' in Figure 7.7 correspond to the production relationship without technical progress and with population expanding at the unconstrained rate $\bar{p}$. If technical progress is insufficient to overcome the impact of diminishing returns ($\delta\bar{p} > s$), YY' will be displaced to some such position as S_1S_1'. A necessary condition for long-run equilibrium is, as before, that the capital–output ratio be constant. In other words, the rate of per capita income growth must be

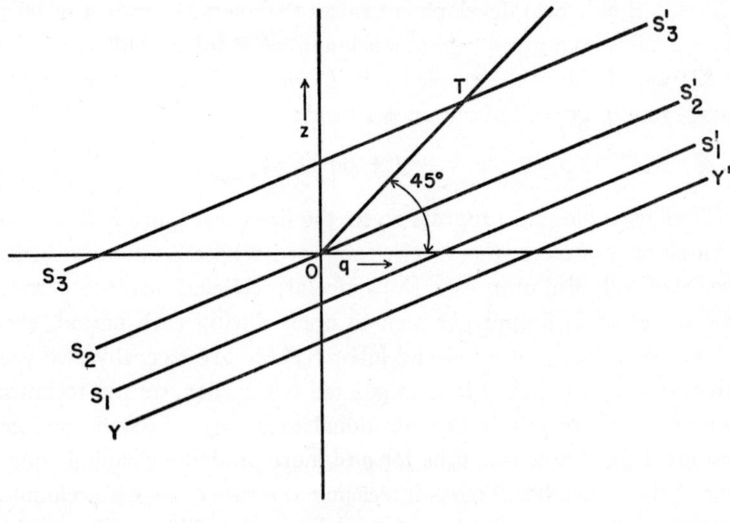

FIG. 7.7

equal to the rate of increase of the capital–labor ratio in equilibrium, It follows from (7.23) that this rate of growth is

$$m = \frac{s - \delta\bar{p}}{1 - \beta} . \tag{7.24}$$

Since $(s - \delta\bar{p}) < 0$, the resultant rates of growth of output per head and of capital per worker are negative.

However, there is no equilibrium in this vicinity, since the declining capital–labor ratio will cause the wage rate to fall to levels at which the population growth rate once again becomes sensitive to changes in wages. The fall in the population growth rate implies a corresponding decrease in the rate of growth of the labor force, and therefore curve S_1S_1' will shift upward. But since, in the new position, the capital–output ratio is still rising, accumulation will decline. Hence the capital–labor ratio will continue to fall, labor growth will continue to decline, and S_1S_1' will continue to shift until the rate of population growth $p = s/\delta$, and S_1S_1' passes through the origin. Under these conditions, the economy will be in long-run equilibrium, because the capital–output ratio is constant and there are no forces in the economy tending to displace it from this position.

This equilibrium is also stable, since, for example, a displacement to the right along S_1S_1' leads to an increase in wages, which increases the rate of growth of the labor force. These effects cause S_1S_1' to be displaced downward, leading to an increase in the capital–output ratio, a decrease in accumulation, a drop in wages, a reduction in population growth, and an eventual return of the economy toward the origin. Similarly, a displacement to the left also gives rise to a set of forces tending to return the economy to the origin.

Thus, the equilibrium position for an economy with decreasing returns despite technical progress is similar to that observed without technical progress except for one important difference: the long-run equilibrium rate of population growth is now positive. This economy, unlike one in a classical stationary state, is not stagnant; it can support an ever-increasing population at a constant standard of living by the fruits of technical progress. The approach to equilibrium in this economy effectively consists of lowering the rate of population growth until the progress of technology can exactly counterbalance the influence of diminishing returns.

If the rate of technical progress should be sufficiently high precisely to overcome the effects of diminishing returns at the unconstrained rate of population growth $\bar{p}$, the effective production function can be represented by S_2S_2'—a line through the origin with a slope β. Under these circumstances, the economy naturally tends toward a golden age in which output, capital, and population are all growing at the same percentage rate $\bar{p} = s/\delta$. A less fortunate economy, like the one of the preceding paragraphs, can reach this stage only by adjusting its rate of technical progress upward or by decreasing, through socio-cultural changes, its unconstrained rate of population growth. From an economic point of view, of course, an economy will be far better off if it can overcome diminishing returns at its unconstrained rate of population growth $\bar{p}$, rather than at a lower rate, since under these circumstances the equilibrium level of per capita income will be higher.

Finally, if at the rate of population growth $\bar{p}$ the technical dynamism of the economy more than offsets the influence of diminishing returns, the production function is shifted to a position like that of S_3S_3', a line whose vertical intercept equals $s - \delta\bar{p}$, where δ is negative. The economy now gravitates toward the equilibrium state represented by T, at which output per head and the capital–labor ratio are rising at the same rate, $m = (s - \delta\bar{p})/(1 - \beta)$, the capital–output ratio is constant, and population is expanding at the unconstrained rate $\bar{p}$. The rate of capital accumulation now required to maintain the capital–output ratio constant is

$$G_n = G_w = \frac{s + \bar{p}\gamma}{1 - \beta}. \tag{7.25}$$

So far our discussion of the effects of technical progress has been based upon the assumption that innovations are, on the average, neutral. If innovations are not neutral, the rate at which the marginal product of capital changes relative to that of labor is altered by technical progress. Capital-using innovations tend to retard the onset of diminishing returns from increases in the capital–labor ratio, and capital-saving innovations tend to accelerate this rate. Graphically, the influence of non-neutral innovations is reflected by a change in the slope of the production curve with technical progress relative to that of YY' in Figure 7.7.[18] Capital-using innovations increase the slope of the production function; capital-saving innovations decrease it. Thus, capital-using innovations tend to shift the point T to the right (since the z-intercept of the production function remains fixed), thereby increasing the equilibrium value of the capital–output ratio and raising the natural rate of growth of capital accordingly.

By the same token, labor-using innovations shift T to the left and reduce the economy's equilibrium capital requirements. Of course, given the slope of the production function, the behavior of the capital–output ratio over time will depend upon the rate of addition to the economy's capital stock.[19] If capital accumulation is persistently insufficient to permit full exploitation of the technological possibilities represented by T, the capital–output ratio will decline and inventions, on the average, will appear to be capital-saving. Should the rate of capital expansion suffice to lead the economy to T, inventions will appear neutral. Otherwise, they will seem to be primarily labor-saving. In the long run, however, the rate of capital accumulation will tend toward the natural rate of growth of capital. That is, accumulation will regulate itself to bring the economy to the point T, and inventions will appear neutral.*

* This may be an explanation of the empirical evidence suggesting neutrality of innovations. This explanation, of course, is based on a once-for-all bias in innovations.

SUMMARY AND CONCLUSIONS

Several conclusions may be drawn from this relatively simple model. First, the most obvious is that the clue to the economy's long-run dynamic behavior may be found in its technical dynamism. Only if the community is sufficiently adaptable to be able to generate a rate of technical progress that exceeds delta times the rate at which its population desires to reproduce can continued improvements in per capita output be achieved in the long run. It should be noted, however, that this required rate of progress is really quite small. For example, if δ were to have the comparatively high value of 0.1 and if net population growth were to take place at 4 per cent per year, a rate of technological progress of only 0.4 per cent per year would be needed to overcome the depressing effect of diminishing returns. (This rate, incidentally, is about one-fifth of the rate in the United States and Great Britain.)

Second, our analysis suggests that the nature of optimal policy with respect to population growth depends upon whether, with constant techniques, production is subject to increasing, constant, or diminishing returns. In an economy with increasing returns to scale, population growth stimulates an additional increase in per capita income; it should therefore be encouraged. In an economy with decreasing returns to scale, on the other hand, population expansion occurs at the cost of a lower rate of improvement of standards of living. In any case, however, this population effect is dwarfed whenever technological progress is significant.

Third, somewhat less apparent is the role played by the character of innovations in determining the nature of the long-run equilibrium position of the economy. As already indicated, a capital-using stream of innovations can result in a higher long-run equilibrium rate of the economy's expansion of the per capita output. Alternatively, these labor-saving innovations can be employed to increase the leisure hours of the working force. Similarly, a succession of labor-using inventions will drive the economy in the opposition direction.

Fourth, while in the long run the rate of accumulation of capital is determined by the natural rate of growth of the economy, its role in the short run is much more significant. Accumulation controls the rate of change of the capital–labor ratio, thereby controlling the rate of change of per capita output. Since the rate of capital accumulation thus determines the point in the $z-q$ plane at which the economy lies, it also affects the time required in the approach of the economy toward its long-run equilibrium position. But a single injection (or a series of isolated injections) of capital into an economy will have no effect on the character of long-run growth. Indeed, the same argument that shows the long-run equilibrium position to be stable can be used to demonstrate that a capital injection generates no forces tending to pull the economy further from its path toward long-run equilibrium.

Of course, whether we can apply the conclusions and deductions we have drawn from our model depends upon the validity of our assumptions. Although our treatment of population is somewhat crude, the results of our analysis are not sensitive to the details of this postulate. Indeed, we could obtain analogous results with any reasonable theory of population growth, exogenous or endogenous.

The second assumption that could conceivably influence the implications of our analysis is full employment. We do not believe that in a practical case small deviations from full employment will significantly affect the results. But, inasmuch as the omission of this postulate would give an additional degree of freedom for the system, it is difficult to make positive assertions. However, the existence of a persistent trend away from full employment (as Marx assumed) would have serious consequences for our results.

More crucial to our conclusions is the assumption that accumulation is positively correlated with the average productivity of capital. Actually, this hypothesis appears reasonable, and in fact it has been built, in one form or another, into all modern models of economic growth.

But there is still one assumption to which our results are quite sensitive: the shape of the production function. This sensitivity exists despite the fact that we have not used the production function to determine the distribution of income between classes (via marginal productivity analysis). Under these circumstances, it is apparent that a careful study of the shape of the production function would be highly desirable before any attempt to apply these conclusions to a particular economic situation is made. Given an appropriate production function, however, analogous reasoning may be used to generate (hopefully) sensible policy recommendations.

EIGHT

SUMMARY AND CONCLUSION

IN THE PRECEDING chapters we have indicated the specific policy implications for economic growth that follow naturally from the work of each author. Let us now see whether a reasonable synthesis of the views of Smith, Ricardo, Marx, Schumpeter, and the moderns can be made to yield a broader set of policy recommendations for speeding economic development.

In order to explore this question it will be helpful to recall the nature of the system with which we have been dealing. The path of real output in our model is determined by the initial state of the economy, the structural interactions within the society, and (possibly) external constraints. As one extreme within our framework, we can postulate an economic system with a sufficient number of interactions among the economic variables to permit the time path of the economy to be determined solely by endogenous forces. In such a model the imposition of any exogenous constraints whatever would overdetermine the system. An economy of this nature has been described in equation form in Chapter Two [equations (2.1) and (2.3)–(2.7)], and its solution for output is

$$(8.1) \qquad Y = Y(K_0, N_0, L_0, S_0, U_0; t; \alpha_1, \ldots, \alpha_j, \ldots) .$$

As in Chapter Two, K_0, N_0, L_0, S_0, U_0 are the initial conditions, α_j are the structural parameters, and t represents the time that has elapsed since the economy was in its initial state.

It is immediately evident from these equations that the task of the economic planner in this society is not at all easy. Not only must he understand in detail the interactions among the several economic variables to estimate quantitatively the effects of his recommendations, but, in addition, his freedom of action is severely limited by the endogenous nature of the system in which he operates. For the value of output at time t cannot be altered unless at least one initial condition or one structural parameter is modified. Moreover, as we saw in Chapter Seven, a change in initial conditions that is not radical enough to influence the economy's structural parameters cannot affect the long-run equilibrium growth rate of per capita output, since the rate of growth of per capita income is determined solely by the structural parameters of the production and population functions and by the growth rate of technology. It follows, then, that a shock that does not alter these parameters cannot increase the long-run rate of economic expansion, regardless of what its short-run effects may be. In particular, such a non-critical shock cannot transform a stagnant economy into one in which self-sustained growth can take place.

Considerations of this sort suggest that the economic planner in such a society may pursue one of two courses of action. On the one hand, by applying an appropriate shock to the system, he can modify its behavior temporarily; the permanent effects of this policy will be found only in the level of operation of the economy. On the other hand, by changing the structural parameters of the system, he can attempt to alter the rate of growth of the economy. This second type of planning activity is considerably more complex than the application of a single shock. The structural parameters of a real economy, which is regularly subjected to randomly directed shocks of varying magnitudes, already reflect the reactions of the system to ordinary exogenous perturbations. Therefore, in order to influence the long-run growth rate of the economy, the planner must either apply an abnormally severe shock to the system, or else impose upon it a persistent series of oriented shocks. For example, suppose that the per capita output of the U.S.S.R. were predicted to exceed that of the United States by 1980. One way to postpone the date of crossover for a few years would be to lower the long-term interest rates in the United States temporarily. But if, instead, the tax structure in the United States were altered to allow permanent substantial tax benefits for the costs of research and development, it is conceivable that the rate of growth of United States per capita output could be made as high as or even higher than that of the U.S.S.R., and the crossover could be eliminated entirely.

In a completely endogenous economy, then, the economic planner's actions appear to be significantly limited. To effect even a temporary change in the course of the economy, he must take forceful action; to alter the long-run path of the system, he must take steps powerful enough to modify the basic behavior of the community; and at all times he must take into account the more or less strong interactions of all parts of the social, cultural, and economic fabric of his society.

At the other end of the spectrum we can postulate an economy within our framework that is ideal for the lazy policy-maker. In this system we assume, for example, that a community exists in which all the economic variables can be specified independently and exogenously. Such a situation probably never arises in real life, except as a transitory phase, but its analysis as a limiting case may prove instructive. Under these circumstances the set of equations (2.1), (2.3)–(2.7) become

$$Y = f(K, N, L, S, U)\,, \tag{8.2}$$

$$K = \overline{K}(t)\,, \tag{8.3}$$

$$N = \overline{N}(t)\,, \tag{8.4}$$

$$L = \overline{L}(t)\,, \tag{8.5}$$

$$S = \overline{S}(t)\,, \tag{8.6}$$

$$U = \overline{U}(t)\,, \tag{8.7}$$

where the functions $\overline{K}$, $\overline{N}$, $\overline{L}$, $\overline{S}$, and $\overline{U}$ are arbitrarily (exogenously) imposed on the system. The solution of these equations for output is, of course,

$$Y = Y(\overline{K}(t), \overline{N}(t), \overline{L}(t), \overline{S}(t), \overline{U}(t)\ ; \alpha_1, \ldots, \alpha_j \ldots)\,. \tag{8.8}$$

In (8.8), the structural parameters α_j originate exclusively in the production function (8.2). Evidently this society imposes no restrictions on the policy-maker other than those implied in (8.2); policy recommendations affecting the time paths of $\overline{K}$, $\overline{N}$, $\overline{L}$, $\overline{S}$, and $\overline{U}$ can be implemented without considering side interactions among these economic variables. If the planner has effective control over the exogenous forces, he can easily direct the future path of the economy and predict its activities even day by day; if he has little influence upon these quantities, he cannot reliably forecast either the economic development of his community or the ultimate effects of his recommendations. In either case, his job is simpler than the planner's job in a completely endogenous society, but it may be more frustrating.

An actual economy, of course, is neither completely endogenous nor completely exogenous. Since the extent to which single or multiple policy goals are attainable depends crucially upon the number and nature of the exogenous constraints and endogenous interactions of the economic variables, it is necessary to investigate further the character of a modern economy. As a step in this direction let us see how much common ground we can find in our five discussions of a capitalist economy on the degree of interdependence of a modern community.

First of all, we note that opinion in chapters Three to Seven is essentially unanimous on the role of "natural resources" in the determination of economic growth. As pointed out in Chapter Two, the term "natural resources" is, by definition, reserved for all the non-reproducible non-exhaustible tangible assets of a community; all its variable natural wealth is considered to be part of its capital stock. As a result, Smith, Ricardo, and Schumpeter specify that each society has a fixed stock of this class of natural endowments that cannot be affected by any economic activity whatever. On the other hand, Marx and the contemporary economists hold that any resource can be improved or degraded, and thus the entire material wealth of the community is more or less exhaustible or reproducible or both. They therefore include all the economic assets of the society in its capital stock, and take "natural resources" as an empty category. From this brief discussion it is evident that none of these authors regard natural resources as an economic variable accessible to policy manipulation.

There is much less unanimity on the nature of the interactions governing the long-run rate of expansion of the employment of labor. All the authors agree that the rate of increase of the labor supply is some function of the rate of population change. Marx and Schumpeter take the rate of population growth to be exogenously determined, whereas Smith, Ricardo, and some of the moderns regard the rate of population expansion as a completely endogenous quantity. Nevertheless, both schools of thought contend that changes in the labor supply place no significant limitations upon the rate of increase of the national product.

According to Marx, the character of innovations is sufficiently labor-displacing to keep the labor market in a chronic state of excess supply. Schumpeter's position is that "development," which is independent of conditions in the labor market, is the major determinant of economic expansion. And the members of the endogenous school argue that the long-run rate of population growth tends to adapt itself to the course of demand in the labor market. In any case, the supply of labor is not an operational policy variable.

Even the demand for labor is not universally agreed to be a fertile field for policy manipulation. In the Marxian model, for example, capitalists automatically maximize the rate of the economy's expansion independently of the (exogenous) changes in population. And in the Schumpeterian system the effects of changes in the employment of labor on long-run total output are dwarfed by comparison with those of technological progress.

When we come to the recommendations of the endogenous school, we find that we must distinguish between measures tending to influence total output and those designed to act upon per capita output. Total output can be altered by changing the employment of labor, since the marginal product of labor is always positive. Because the supply of labor is adaptive, the employment of labor can be increased secularly only by expanding the demand for labor. This can be accomplished either by injecting capital or by changing somehow the rate of expansion of the economy.

By contrast, the policy recommendations for per capita output depend crucially upon the technical character of returns to scale. In an economy in which production is subject to permanently increasing returns, per capita output will expand more rapidly, as we saw in Chapter Seven, if the rate of population expansion is raised. According to the endogenous school, population growth can be stimulated directly by reducing subsistence wages through the introduction of cost-reducing innovations in agriculture and in appropriate consumer-goods industries. A similar argument for an economy with decreasing returns to scale suggests that an actual reduction in population would lead to increased per capita output. In such an economy, then, population growth should be inhibited by such actions as policy-induced changes in cultural values aimed at reducing the birth rate and at raising the universally acceptable standard of living.

We now come to the third of the three basic factors of production: capital accumulation. In general, we find that the rate of capital formation is regarded as endogenous and determined by both the ability to save and the incentives to save and invest. Since wages are by and large entirely consumed, the ability to save is considered to be a function of total profits (or of some similar quantity). The incentive to invest, on the other hand, is normally taken to be a function of the rate of return on investment, net of compensation for the trouble of investment and for the risk involved.

In the classical system there is no distinction between desired savings and planned investment, even in the short run. The supply of savings is automatically in balance with the demand for investment capital. This does not imply, however, that the investment and savings motives are on a par. Ricardo and Marx felt that the drive to invest is the dominant influence, whereas Smith felt that the desire to achieve some particular level of consumption in the future plays the paramount role.

Schumpeter and the moderns agree with Ricardo. They recognize, of course, that, in the short run, *ex ante* savings need not equal *ex ante* investment. But, in the long run, they believe that the ability to save follows the incentive to invest. Hence, the weight of opinion appears to be that it is not the lack of savings capacity that explains the low rate of accumulation in underdeveloped areas; it is rather a scarcity of profitable investment outlets.

In order to increase the rate of accumulation, then, a planner ought to enhance the drive to invest by reducing the risks of capital investment and by operating upon the determinants of net profit. Both Smith and Ricardo, for example, argued for the creation of a political and legal environment favorable to business activity. As steps in this direction, Smith recommended measures to regulate competition, to ensure freedom of international trade, and to legalize lending operations, as well as general measures to increase the security of life and property. Although Schumpeter would support these recommendations, he would still argue against those risk-reducing measures that might simultaneously decrease the rate of innovation. The institution of a 100 per cent reserve requirement, for example, might reduce investment risks by damping price level fluctuations. But, since it would also destroy the ability of banks to create new credit to finance entrepreneurial activity, a step of this nature is more likely to decrease investment than to increase it.

All our authors agree that a change in the profit rate influences the rate of capital formation; they disagree about the direction of the effect. Smith, for example, maintains that investment is undertaken by capitalists because they need a specific level of income from the use of their capital stock. When profit rates decrease, therefore, they must extend their investment activities to retain their standard of living. For Marx the investment arises more from the need to compete, which introduces capital-intensive, cost-reducing innovations that respond to a decline in the rate of profit. Both authors, therefore, visualize a negatively sloped supply curve of capital as a function of its marginal efficiency.

According to Ricardo, Schumpeter, and the moderns, the incentive to invest is really the lure of high profits, and hence they contend that the supply curve of capital has a positive slope. Because they disagree on the fundamental nature of the variation of investment rate with the rate of net profit, it is not possible to extract from their writings any universally acceptable policy for the direction of profit rate changes.

Nevertheless, since the key to accumulation lies in the rate of profit, we must still investigate the mechanism of its determination. Here, too, our economists disagree. Smith says that the rate of profit net of risk is fixed by the capital stock and the institutional structure of the economy. Since he also assumes that a larger capital stock can be employed only at a lower marginal rate of return, accumulation in a Smithian economy can be accelerated during the approach to the stationary state by injections of capital. In the process, the advent of the stationary state itself is also speeded up.

Ricardo says that the rate of profit is independent of the capital stock. Indeed, it is not influenced by any economic characteristics other than the level of subsistence wages. In his system the rate of profit can be increased only by lowering the subsistence wage. Thus Ricardo recommends increased agricultural productivity and the importation of food as two measures to step up the pace of capital accumulation. He does not recommend, for example, socio-culturally induced reductions in subsistence standards, since such a policy would lead to an increased population, which, in turn, would decrease per capita incomes in the stationary state.

In a Marxian economy, the character of innovations has the greatest influence on the rate of profit (assuming, with Marx, that the rate of exploitation of labor is kept as high as possible). As pointed out in Chapter Five, Marx is inconsistent in his discussion of the historical path of the rate of return; nonetheless, he is correct in maintaining that capital-using innovations will lead to a declining rate of profit in the event that a sufficiently large share of the resultant productivity gains is appropriated by labor in the form of increased real wages.

For Schumpeter it is not the character of the innovations, but their quantity that is important. Schumpeterian profits, and hence Schumpeterian accumulation, depend solely and crucially upon the rate of technical progress. There can be neither a drying up of sources of investment capital nor a decline of investment opportunities so long as innovations continue at a sufficiently high rate. To stimulate profits and accumulation, then, Schumpeter would create an economic and political environment conducive to rapid technological progress.

The moderns, too, emphasize the importance of technological developments in the determination of the rates of profit and accumulation. We have seen that in the long run the course of the profit rate of the economy depends upon the nature of returns to scale. During the approach to the long-run equilibrium state the average rate of profit rises secularly, and accumulation proceeds at an ever-increasing rate whenever production is subject to increasing returns. On the other hand, when returns to scale are either constant or diminishing, the profit rate and hence the rate of capital formation decline as the economy moves toward equilibrium. Since appropriate technical progress can make an economy with constant or diminishing returns to scale behave like one with increasing returns, the encouragement of innovations is a major recommendation of policy planners of the modern school.

Generally speaking, our authors are far from united on the determinants of the rate of profit, but they would all agree that both technological progress and the reduction of risk must be encouraged in order to speed up accumulation in an underdeveloped economy.

The subject of technological change, unlike that of the three usual factors of production, approaches the borderline between economics and the other social sciences, and hence its analysis is in a much less satisfactory state than that of capital, labor, and national resources. Naturally, one determinant of the growth rate of a community's applied scientific, technical, and organizational knowledge is the increase of knowledge itself. But the mere existence of additional technical knowledge does not necessarily and automatically advance the state of productive efficiency. Rather, it is generally agreed that the growth of knowledge is autonomous; however, its incorporation into the productive process may depend on other features of the economy. The usual view is that there always exists an excess supply of untapped inventions that can be exploited under appropriate economic conditions. It then follows that industrial innovations are much more likely to result from the application of existing techniques than from new research. This suggests that the rate of innovations in most societies is not limited by a lack of technical knowledge, but by some other characteristic of the economy.

Ricardo (happily) and most moderns (more or less reluctantly) assume that the rate of innovation is exogenously specified. Smith and Marx, on the other hand, assume that it is a monotonically increasing function of the community's rate of accumulation; Smith says that it is capitalist rationality, and Marx that it is cutthroat competition, that forces the capitalist to exploit the best possible techniques of production.

A third and rather different view is held by Schumpeter. He argues that the tendency to adopt improved techniques is not an automatic concomitant of accumulation; rather, it is a measure (by definition) of entrepreneurial activity. The rate at which new techniques are incorporated into the productive process depends strongly on the reaction of the socio-cultural environment to entrepreneurial efforts and on the willingness of the society to develop, employ, and reward entrepreneurial talent. The availability of savings is neither a necessary nor a sufficient condition for technical progress, but the extent to which credit institutions will supply the potential innovator with claims upon the factors of production will help determine the rate at which new methods of production are adopted.

In today's world, we cannot satisfactorily maintain that technological progress is exogenous, particularly since it interacts with the rate of capital accumulation. We shall therefore disregard this possibility in our attempt to distill a consensus on the factors that determine the rate of technological progress.

The more or less classical position, that innovations are automatically adopted and are limited only by current accumulation, appears to ignore the strong influence that socio-cultural (and particularly political) conditions can exert on the rate of improvement of productive efficiency. On the other hand, as Schumpeter himself recognized, the use of credit to finance new investment is inherently inflationary during the interval between the investment and the resultant flow of output. In the context of economic development, the relatively long gestation period may lead to an unacceptable degree and duration of inflation. Thus, to the extent that it is desired to achieve technological progress without undue price level fluctuations, the rate of introducing innovations must be geared to the current rate of savings. Two recommendations more or less in accord with the views of Smith, Marx, and Schumpeter would therefore be (1) to set up or strengthen appropriate financial institutions which can mobilize savings and transform them into venture capital, and (2) to encourage those changes in the socio-cultural milieu that will permit more rapid acceptance of technical change.

Like technical progress, the socio-cultural environment, the last of our five socio-economic variables, is not strictly an economic quantity. Nevertheless, we must still investigate our authors' views on the determinants of this important but elusive variable. The classical school and the moderns both assume that the evolution of the social, political, cultural, and institutional structure of the community is exogenous, and is therefore somewhat amenable to independent policy manipulation. Marx and Schumpeter, on the other hand, contend that endogenous constraints upon the path of this socio-cultural variable do exist and that they take the form of interrelationships between its components and those of the technological vector. Where Marx disagrees with Schumpeter is in the direction of causation. For Marx, the relations of production (i.e., technology, in the broad sense) determine the character of the society. Schumpeter is not so sure, and basically believes that the relationship between socio-cultural factors and technology is an implicit one. Since it is possible to see many examples throughout history of technology's influence on culture and vice versa, Schumpeter's position appears to be the sounder.

In any case, the policy implications are clear. If the socio-cultural environment is exogenous, it can be edged in directions that are consistent with the economic planner's policy goals and value judgments.

If the socio-cultural environment is endogenous, we find that our real-life economy is basically the endogenous model discussed at the beginning of this chapter, in which a policy decision with respect to any variable in the system will have repercussions throughout the entire community.

In summary, we find first of all that, if we accept the more reasonable features of the several analyses considered in the earlier chapters of this book, we are led to the point of view that the economic evolution of a community is most appropriately described by an essentially completely endogenous system of interrelated equations. The only exogenous quantity is the empty category of "natural resources." We must conclude, therefore, that there is no simple explanation for underdevelopment. Underdevelopment cannot be ascribed solely to a deficiency of capital, or to a lack of entrepreneurial talent, or to an adverse population-to-resources ratio, or to a hostile institutional environment. By the same token, a vicious-circle argument that focuses upon a single relationship, such as the savings–income function or the innovation–entrepreneurship identity, cannot furnish a completely valid explanation of underdevelopment. The phenomenon of underdevelopment must be understood, rather, in the context of the entire complex of interrelationships that characterize the economic and social life of the community.

This non-partitionable character of a modern underdeveloped economy has another important consequence. Since the system also has strong stability features, as discussed in Chapter Seven, it follows that long-run changes in the rate of growth of per capita output cannot be induced unless at least one structural parameter of the economy is modified. To generate economic development, then, one must impose upon the society shocks that are large enough to alter its behavioral patterns significantly. Our synthesis of the views of the several authors analyzed in this book, therefore, supports the "critical minimum effort" thesis of Leibenstein,[1] which states, in effect, that there is a threshold for practical economic stimulants to development. In other words, our analysis suggests that, in general, the gradualist approach to economic development is unlikely to be successful.

We can also make several recommendations about the nature of economic development itself. In Chapter One we defined economic development as the process by which an economy whose rate of growth of per capita income is small or negative is transformed into an economy in which a significant, self-sustained rate of increase of per capita income is a permanent long-run feature. Hence, in view of the discussion of Chapter Seven, a necessary condition for economic development is that the production function of the society, including the effects of technological progress, be subject to increasing returns to scale. Otherwise, permanent sustained growth of per capita income is not possible (at least in the absence of permanent exogenous stimuli).

Since technological progress is more likely to be continuous and systematic in manufacturing than in agricultural pursuits, and since greater economies of scale are ultimately to be found there,[2] it follows that industrialization must be an important part of any successful development program. Similarly, the greater economies of scale in heavy manufacturing (as opposed to light industry)[3] suggest that "basic" industries, such as metals and investment goods in general, ought to be emphasized. However, as Ricardo pointed out, the close relationship between manufacturing wages and the cost of subsistence requires that the process of industrialization be preceded by or accompanied by a rise in agricultural productivity.

Obviously, little industralization of an underdeveloped country can take place unless it is closely associated with significant technical and socio-cultural changes in the community. Industrialization, however, is not the only reason for the inseparability of such changes from development processes. As we have seen, in order to encourage economic growth in a non-developing economy, one must create economic and social conditions in which any potential economies of scale can become effective. Some appropriate combination of technical and institutional change would therefore appear to be the direct means of modifying the relevant structural parameters of the production function.

This conclusion is strengthened by two additional arguments. First, the nature of the functional relationship between technical progress and socio-cultural change indicates that the effects of modifying the socio-technical environment tend to be cumulative. For example, structural changes such as urbanization tend to reduce dependence upon traditional value systems and thereby to increase popular receptivity to unfamiliar knowledge, values, and skills. The spread of new patterns and relationships, in turn, leads to additional stimulation of social, cultural, and technological progress.

Second, since all our authors agree that both the rate of change of the employment of labor and the rate of capital accumulation tend to be adaptive, a shock on either L or K must be quite large before it can affect the structural parameters of the production function. This implies that even large shocks on L or K, without corresponding stimulation of technical and socio-cultural change, constitute relatively inefficient modes of influencing the long-term rate of growth of the community. Both by direct argument and by elimination, then, we must assign to the technical and socio-cultural variables the role of prime movers in the *initiation* of economic development.

This does not mean, of course, that increased investment is not crucial to the take-off process. On the contrary, since all but organizational innovations require some fresh capital for their implementation, new investment will be needed to initiate technical change. However, the new capital will be effective in the long run only if it draws heavily upon new techniques. Thus, an emphasis on demonstration projects and pilot-plant operations seems to be indicated, since these types of investments are likely to result in much greater long-run benefits than the mere duplication of existing facilities.

The identification of development with the creation of systematic conditions of increasing returns to scale also suggests that the provision of overhead capital may serve an important function in the consolidation and amplification of the gains of the initial stages of economic development. Specifically, the construction of a transportation system and other public utilities, investment in education, and improvements in public health are three significant sources of external economies. It follows from our discussion, therefore, that investment in social capital should not be neglected in any over-all development plan.

A careful consideration of the analysis of this chapter suggests strongly that governmental agencies must play an active role in planning and initiating economic development. First of all, the government is a vital institution for the introduction of purposive socio-cultural and technical change. Second, investment in social capital will not generally be undertaken by private investors. Third, a government has the power to establish a tax and fiscal system that can divert resources into those sectors of the economy that are most capable of systematic exploitation of increasing returns and technological innovations. Finally, we must recognize that in the real world the resources available for development are normally far too scarce to permit simultaneous implementation of all our recommendations. From a purely economic view, then, it would appear that vigorous governmental leadership and direction are necessary for the successful modernization of the economic and social life of a nation.

NOTES

The following abbreviations are used in the Notes:

A-D—Friedrich Engels, *Anti-Dühring,* translated and reprinted in E. Burns, *A Handbook of Marxism* (London: Gollancz, 1935).
BC—J. A. Schumpeter, *Business Cycles* (New York: McGraw-Hill, 1939).
Cap, I—Karl Marx, *Capital,* translated from the third German edition by S. Moore and E. Aveling, revised according to the fourth German edition by E. Untermann (Chicago: Kerr & Co., 1906), Volume I.
Cap, II—Karl Marx, *Capital,* translated from the second German edition by E. Untermann (Chicago: Kerr & Co., 1909), Volume II.
Cap, III—Karl Marx, *Capital,* translated from the first German edition by E. Untermann (Chicago: Kerr & Co., 1909), Volume III.
CSD—J. A. Schumpeter, *Capitalism, Socialism and Democracy,* 3d ed. (New York: Harper, 1950).
PS—Piero Sraffa (ed.), *David Ricardo: Works and Correspondence,* 10 Vols. (Cambridge: Cambridge University Press, 1953).
R—David Ricardo, *The Principles of Political Economy and Taxation* (London: Dent and Son, 1937).

NOTES TO CHAPTER ONE

1. Harvey Leibenstein, *Economic Backwardness and Economic Growth* (New York: Wiley, 1957), pp. 38–45.
2. L. W. Shannon, *Underdeveloped Areas* (New York: Harper and Bros., 1957), p. 11.
3. For a more thorough discussion of the problems involved see Adamantios Pepelasis, Leon Mears, and Irma Adelman, *Economic Development: Analysis and Case Studies* (New York: Harper and Bros., 1961), Chapter I.
4. Simon Kuznets, "National Income and Industrial Structure," *Econometrica,* XVII (1949), 215–20.
5. Milton Gilbert and I. G. Kravis, "Empirical Problems in International Comparisons of National Product," *Income and Wealth,* Series IV (London, 1955), pp. 115–19.
6. For a definition of the concepts of structure, theory, and model, see A. G. Papandreou, *Economics as a Science* (Philadelphia: Lippincott, 1959), pp. 56–120.

NOTES TO CHAPTER TWO

1. Another possible criterion of comparative economic performance is the size of the potential economic surplus. See Paul Baran, *The Political Economy of Growth* (New York: Monthly Review Press, 1957), p. 22.

2. For a discussion of the definition of the term "state of technical knowledge," see Joan Robinson, "The Production Function and the Theory of Capital," *Review of Economic Studies,* XXI, No. 2 (1953–54), 90–93.

3. Schumpeter, for example, writes: "It is not possible to explain *economic* change by previous *economic* conditions alone. For the economic state of a people does not emerge from the preceding economic conditions, but only from the preceding total situation." J. A. Schumpeter, *The Theory of Economic Development* (Cambridge, Mass.: Harvard University Press, 1949), p. 58.

4. For recent discussions of these difficulties, see Joan Robinson, *The Accumulation of Capital* (London: Macmillan, 1956), pp. 114–23, and "The Production Function and the Theory of Capital," *Review of Economic Studies,* XXI, No. 2 (1953–54), 81–106; D. G. Champernowne and R. F. Kahn, "The Value of Invested Capital," *Review of Economic Studies,* XXI, No. 2 (1953–54), 107–11; Champernowne, "The Production Function and the Theory of Capital, A Comment," *Review of Economic Studies,* XXI, No. 2 (1953–54), 112–35; and R. M. Solow, "The Production Function and the Theory of Capital," *Review of Economic Studies,* XXIII, No. 2 (1955–56), 101–8.

5. See Robinson, *The Accumulation of Capital,* p. 113.

6. Harvey Leibenstein, *Economic Backwardness and Economic Growth* (New York: Wiley, 1957), p. 20.

7. Difficulties of measurement of labor are discussed in Robinson, *The Accumulation of Capital,* p. 117.

8. A similar index is also introduced by Trygve Haavelmo, *A Study in the Theory of Economic Evolution* (Amsterdam: North Holland Publishing Co., 1954), p. 46.

9. For a discussion of the importance of U_t in economic development, see J. J. Spengler, "Sociological Value Theory, Economic Analysis and Economic Policy," *American Economic Review, Papers and Proceedings,* XLIII (May 1953), 340–49; M. Gottlieb, "The Theory of an Economic System," *American Economic Review, Papers and Proceedings,* XLIII (May 1953), 360–63; and A. O. Hirschman, *The Strategy of Economic Development* (New Haven: Yale University Press, 1958).

10. Cf. Haavelmo, *Economic Evolution,* pp. 45–63.

11. For a discussion of several crucial structural parameters, see W. W. Rostow, *The Process of Economic Growth,* 2d ed. (New York: Norton, 1960).

12. This is the point of Leibenstein, *Economic Backwardness,* Chapter I.

NOTES TO CHAPTER THREE

1. Adam Smith, *The Wealth of Nations* (New York: Random House, 1937), p. 53. (Subsequent numbers refer to pages of this edition.)

2. 53. 3. 242–47. 4. 7. 5. 17. 6. 260. 7. 421. 8. 260. 9. 421. 10. 260.

11. 145. 12. 79; subsequent quotations and references, 79–81. 13. 69.

14. 69. 15. 69. 16. 81. 17. This and subsequent quotations, 321. 18. 268 (italics ours). 19. 355. 20. 347.

21. 48 (italics ours); cf. also 262. 22. 421. 23. 93. 24. 37. 25. 336. 26. 336; cf. also 112 and 249–50. 27. 250, 118. 28. 111. 29. 96. 30. 118–43.

31. 339–40. 32. 96; cf. also 94. 33. 93; subsequent quotations and references, 93–95. 34. 70–71; 92–93. 35. 20. 36. 73. 37. 94. 38. 94–95. 39. 95. 40. 95.

41. 73. 42. 326. 43. 425 ff. 44. 423.

NOTES TO CHAPTER FOUR

1. David Ricardo, *The Principles of Political Economy and Taxation* (London: Dent and Son, 1937), pp. 35–37. (Hereafter R.)

2. R 35. 3. R 36. 4. R 52 (italics ours). 5. R 52. 6. R 56.

7. Piero Sraffa (ed.), *David Ricardo: Works and Correspondence,* 10 Vols. (Cambridge: Cambridge University Press, 1953), I, 61. (This edition hereafter PS.) Cf. also R 270, and Paul Samuelson, "A Modern Treatment of the Ricardian Economy," *Quarterly Journal of Economics,* LXXIV (May 1959), 218.

8. R 33. 9. R 35. 10. R 52. 11. R 55. 12. R 53. 13. R 55. 14. R 52. 15. R 54–55. 16. R 53. 17. R 53, 57. 18. R 54. 19. R 53. 20. R 53.

21. R 71. 22. R 56. 23. R 80. 24. R 56. 25. R 61. 26. R 70. 27. R 53. 28. R 79; cf. also 95. 29. R 73. 30. R 266–67.

31. PS, IX, 193. 32. R 73, 266. 33. R 193. 34. R 193. 35. R 73. 36. R 281. 37. R 41. 38. R 70.

39. PS, VI, 147. I am indebted to E. V. McKinley, "The Theory of Economic Development in the English Classical School" (unpublished doctoral dissertation, University of California, Berkeley, 1954) for this interpretation.

40. R 76.

41. Ricardo recognized the need for this proviso. See his *Notes on Malthus—Principles of Political Economy* (Baltimore: Johns Hopkins University Press, 1928), p. lxxiii.

42. R 71–75. 43. R 55. 44. R 73–75. 45. R 55–57. 46. R 71. 47. R 55. 48. R 72. 49. R 71. 50. R 57. 51. R 63.

52. This and subsequent quotations and references, R 56.

NOTES TO CHAPTER FIVE

1. William Fellner, "Marxian Hypotheses and Observable Trends Under Capitalism: A 'Modernized' Interpretation," *Economic Journal,* LXVII (1957), 22.

2. Karl Marx, *Capital,* translated from the third German edition by S. Moore and E. Aveling, revised according to the fourth German edition

by E. Untermann (Chicago: Kerr & Co., 1906), I, 197–98. (Hereafter *Cap*, I.)

3. *Cap*, I, 197. **4.** *Cap*, I, 83. **5.** *Cap*, I, 199. **6.** *Cap*, I, 562.

7. See, for example, Karl Marx, *A Critique of Political Economy*, translated by N. I. Stone (Chicago: Kerr & Co., 1904), pp. 268, 273–74.

8. M. M. Bober, *Karl Marx's Interpretation of History* (Cambridge, Mass.: Harvard University Press, 1950), p. 24.

9. Marx, *Critique*, p. 11.

10. Friedrich Engels, *Anti-Dühring*, translated and reprinted in E. Burns, *A Handbook of Marxism* (London: Gollancz, 1935), p. 279. (Hereafter *A-D*.)

11. Karl Marx, *The Poverty of Philosophy* (London: Lawrence and Wishart, 1956), pp. 122–23.

12. *A-D* 266.

13. Friedrich Engels, *Ludwig Feuerbach*, translated and reprinted in E. Burns, *A Handbook of Marxism*, p. 225.

14. *A-D* 257. **15.** Marx, *Critique*, p. 11. **16.** *A-D* 257. **17.** *A-D* 279.

18. Friedrich Engels, *The Origin of the Family, Private Property and the State*, translated and reprinted in Burns, *Handbook of Marxism*, p. 315.

19. *Ibid.*, p. 317.

20. *Ibid.* **21.** *Ibid.*, pp. 320 ff. **22.** *A-D* 270. **23.** *A-D* 280–81. **24.** *Cap*, I, 785–86. **25.** *Cap*, I, 818. **26.** *Cap*, I, 836. **27.** *Cap*, I, 837.

28. Henri Sée, *The Economic Interpretation of History*, translated by M. M. Knight (New York: Adelphi, 1929), pp. 115, 113.

29. Joan Robinson, *An Essay on Marxian Economics* (London: Macmillan, 1957), p. 6.

30. Karl Marx, "Theories of Surplus Value," *Selections*, translated by G. A. Bonner and E. Burns (London: Lawrence and Wishart, 1951), p. 329.

31. Cf., e.g., *Cap*, I, Chap. 25. **32.** *Ibid.* **33.** *Cap*, I, 689. **34.** *Cap*, I, 671. **35.** Robinson, *Marxian Economics*, p. 8.

36. This and subsequent quotations, *Cap*, I, 682. **37.** *Cap*, I, 241.

38. *Cap*, I, 568 ff. (however, he is inconsistent on the latter point). **39.** *Cap*, I, 696–97. **40.** *Cap*, I, 690.

41. *Cap*, I, 699; see also P. M. Sweezy, *The Theory of Capitalist Development* (New York: Oxford University Press, 1942), p. 86.

42. *Cap*, I, 701–2. **43.** *Cap*, I, 693. **44.** *Cap*, I, 694–95. **45.** *Cap*, I, 699. **46.** *Cap*, I, 701. **47.** *Cap*, I, 190. **48.** *Cap*, I, 190; cf. also Robinson, *Marxian Economics*, p. 35. **49.** *Cap*, I, 708, 707. **50.** *Cap*, I, 709.

51. Karl Marx and Friedrich Engels, *The Communist Manifesto*, ed. by S. H. Beer (New York: Appleton-Century-Crofts, 1953), p. 22.

52. *Cap*, I, 708–9.

53. This is the interpretation of Karl Kautzky, "Verelendung und Zusammenbruch," *Die Neue Zeit*, XXV (1908).

54. For a more thorough discussion of this point, see Bober, *Marx's Interpretation of History*, pp. 213–21.

55. Thomas Sowell, "Marx's 'Increasing Misery' Doctrine," *American Economic Review*, L (March 1960), 111–20.

56. *Cap*, I, 656. 57. *Cap*, I, 657. 58. *Cap*, I, 662. 59. *Cap*, I, 667. 60. This and subsequent quotations, *Cap*, I, 648–52. 61. *Cap*, I, 684–85.

62. Karl Marx, "Wage-Labour and Capital," reprinted in *Marx and Engels Selected Works* (Moscow: Foreign Language Publishing House, 1955), Vol. I, pp. 99–100 (italics in text).

63. Karl Marx, *Capital*, translated from the first German edition by E. Untermann (Chicago: Kerr & Co., 1909), III, 247–50. (Hereafter *Cap*, III.)

64. *Cap*, III, 248. 65. *Cap*, I, 662.

66. For two excellent discussions of this point, see Robinson, *Marxian Economics*, pp. 41–49, and Sweezy, *Capitalist Development*, pp. 100–108.

67. *Cap*, III, 264. 68. *Cap*, III, 283. 69. *Cap*, III, 300–301. 70. *Cap*, III, 299. 71. *Cap*, III, 283. 72. *Cap*, I, 686. 73. *Cap*, I, 637. 74. *Cap*, I, 688–89. 75. *Cap*, III, 299.

76. Cf., e.g., *Cap*, III, 293. 77. Cf., e.g., *Cap*, III, 310, 312, 516. 78. *Cap*, III, 292.

79. Karl Marx, *Capital*, translated from the second German edition by E. Untermann (Chicago: Kerr & Co., 1909), II, 524–25. (Hereafter *Cap*, II.) See especially Chapters 20 and 21.

80. *Cap*, II, 571–85, especially p. 578. 81. *Cap*, II, 571–72. 82. *Cap*, III, Chap. 15.

83. *Cap*, III, 287; see also Robinson, *Marxian Economics*, for further discussion of Marx's cyclical theory.

84. *Cap*, III, 286. 85. *Cap*, III, 287. 86. *Cap*, III, 293. 87. Marx and Engels, *Communist Manifesto*, pp. 15–16, 22.

88. Karl Marx, "The British Rule in India," *The New York Tribune*, June 25, 1853; reprinted in Burns, *A Handbook of Marxism*, p. 182.

89. *Ibid.*, p. 184. 90. *Ibid.*, p. 187. 91. *Ibid.*, pp. 182 ff. 92. Marx, "British Rule," p. 184. 93. *Ibid.*, p. 182.

94. Karl Marx, "The Future Results of British Rule in India," *New York Tribune*, August 8, 1853; reprinted in Burns, *Handbook*.

95. See, e.g., Robert Ozanne, "Impact of Unions on Wage Levels and Income Distribution," *Quarterly Journal of Economics*, LXXIII (May 1959), 188.

96. Nicolas Kaldor, "A Model of Economic Growth," *Economic Journal*, LXVII (1957), 592.

97. William Fellner, "Marxian Hypotheses," *Economic Journal*, LXVII (1957), 22–24.

98. Ozanne, "Impact of Unions," p. 186.

99. Fellner, "Marxian Hypotheses," p. 24.

100. J. S. Bain, *Industrial Organization* (New York: Wiley, 1959), pp. 197–201.

101. R. J. Lampman, "Recent Changes in Income Inequality Reconsidered," *American Economic Review*, XLIV (June 1954), 251–69.

102. Joan Robinson, "Marx, Marshall and Keynes," *The Delhi School of Economics*, Occasional Paper No. 9 (1955), p. 27.

103. See, e.g., Joan Robinson, *The Accumulation of Capital* (London: Macmillan, 1956) for a continuation of Marx's analysis on this point.

104. R. F. Harrod, "An Essay in Dynamic Theory," *Economic Journal* (March 1939), pp. 19–33.

105. E. D. Domar, "Capital Expansion, Rate of Growth and Employment," *Econometrica,* XIV (April 1946), pp. 137–47.

106. Harvey Leibenstein, *Economic Backwardness and Economic Growth* (New York: Wiley, 1957).

107. Robinson, "Marx, Marshall and Keynes," p. 12.

NOTES TO CHAPTER SIX

1. See, e.g., E. S. Mason, "Monopoly and the Large Firm," in S. E. Harris, *Schumpeter, Social Scientist* (Cambridge, Mass.: Harvard University Press, 1951), p. 93.

2. J. A. Schumpeter, *The Theory of Economic Development,* translated by R. Opie (Cambridge, Mass.: Harvard University Press, 1949), p. 15. (Hereafter *T*.) First German edition in 1912.

3. *T* 17.

4. *T* 16. Cf. also J. A. Schumpeter, *Business Cycles* (New York: McGraw-Hill, 1939), Vol. I, pp. 38, 74. (Hereafter *BC*.)

5. *T* 11. 6. *T* 11. 7. *T* 58. 8. *BC* 74. 9. *T* 63 and footnote. 10. *T* 68. 11. *BC* 83. 12. *T* 64 n (italics in original). 13. *BC* 74. 14. *BC* 74.

15. *T* 68. 16. *T* 68 n. 17. *BC* 74. 18. *BC* 75. 19. *BC* 81. 20. *BC* 79. 21. *BC* 83. 22. *T* 154. 23. *T* 154. 24. *BC* 84.

25. *T* 58 (italics in original). 26. *T* 65–66. 27. *T* 66. 28. *T* 74. 29. *T* 75. 30. *T* 77. 31. *T* 88–89. 32. *T* 78. 33. *T* 93.

34. J. A. Schumpeter, *Capitalism, Socialism and Democracy,* 3d ed. (New York: Harper, 1950), p. 124. (Hereafter *CSD*.)

35. *CSD* 123. 36. *CSD* 110. 37. *T* 88.

38. *T* 122. For a good discussion of this point, see R. J. Wolfson, "The Economic Dynamics of Joseph Schumpeter," *Economic Development and Cultural Change,* XII (October 1958), 31–53.

39. *T* 116. 40. *T* 117. 41. *T* 106–7. 42. *T* 108. 43. *T* 110. 44. *T* 223. 45. *T* 228. 46. *T* 228. 47. *T* 228–29. 48. *T* 229. 49. *T* 230.

50. *T* 231. 51. *T* 232–35. 52. *T* 242–43. 53. *CSD* 68. 54. *CSD* 118. 55. *CSD* 161–62. 56. *CSD* 131–34. 57. *CSD* 139–42. 58. *CSD* 134–39. 59. *CSD* 139. 60. *CSD* 156–61. 61. *CSD* 143–55. 62. *CSD* 162.

NOTES TO CHAPTER SEVEN

1. Some of the major recent contributions to the analysis of growth and development are: R. F. Harrod, *Towards a Dynamic Economics* (London: Macmillan, 1959); Joan Robinson, *The Accumulation of Capital* (London: Macmillan, 1956); Harvey Leibenstein, *Economic Backwardness and Economic Growth* (New York: Wiley, 1957); J. S. Dusenberry, *Business Cycles and Economic Growth* (New York: McGraw-Hill, 1958); D. G. Champernowne, "Capital Accumulation and the Maintenance of Full Em-

ployment," *Economic Journal,* LXVIII (June 1958), 211–45; Nicolas Kaldor, "A Model of Economic Growth," *Economic Journal,* LXVII (December 1957), 591–624; I. M. D. Little, "Classical Growth," *Oxford Economic Papers* (N.S.), IX (June 1957), 152–77; J. H. Power, "The Economic Framework of a Theory of Growth," *Economic Journal,* LXVII (March 1958), 34–51; T. W. Swan, "Economic Growth and Capital Accumulation," *Economic Record,* XXXII (November 1956), 334–61; Robert Solow, "A Contribution to the Theory of Economic Growth," *Quarterly Journal of Economics,* LXV (February 1956), 65–94; James Tobin, "A Dynamic Aggregative Model," *Journal of Political Economy,* LXIII (April 1955), 103–15.

2. For a similar assumption, see Robinson, *The Accumulation of Capital,* pp. 68–69.

3. This postulate is also introduced by Leibenstein in *Economic Backwardness,* p. 20.

4. A similar postulate is made by Harrod, *Dynamic Economics,* pp. 74–80.

5. See Nicolas Kaldor, "Alternative Theories of Distribution," *Review of Economic Studies,* XXIII (March 1956), 94–100.

6. See Chapter Five. The same postulate is introduced by Michael Kalecki, *Theory of Economic Dynamics* (London: Allen and Unwin, 1954), p. 53, and by Robinson, *The Accumulation of Capital,* pp. 73–76, among others. It is validated empirically in an unpublished study by H. Houthakker.

7. See Champernowne, "Capital Accumulation," pp. 216–17.

8. Harrod, *Dynamic Economics,* pp. 81–82.

9. Cf. Kaldor, "A Model of Economic Growth," pp. 611–12; and Champernowne, "Capital Accumulation," pp. 217–18.

10. Harrod, *Dynamic Economics,* pp. 87–94.

11. Robinson, *Accumulation of Capital,* pp. 99–100.

12. Alan Young, "Increasing Returns and Economic Progress," *Economic Journal,* XXXVIII (December 1928), 527–42.

13. *Ibid.,* p. 534.

14. This graph resembles that given by Kaldor, "A Model of Economic Growth," p. 609, for the case of technical progress.

15. This is in accord with Kaldor, "A Model of Economic Growth," p. 611.

16. Cf. Swan, "Economic Growth," p. 334.

17. See Kaldor, "Economic Growth," pp. 595–96.

18. Cf. Swan, "Economic Growth," p. 338 footnote.

19. Kaldor, "Economic Growth," p. 597.

NOTES TO CHAPTER EIGHT

1. Harvey Leibenstein, *Economic Backwardness and Economic Growth* (New York: Wiley, 1947), p. 99.

2. H. B. Chenery, "Interindustry Research in Economic Development," *American Economic Review, Papers and Proceedings* (May 1960) pp. 649–53.

3. *Ibid.*

INDEX

INDEX